David-
unleash up
greatness!

HOW TO CREATE LIFETIME CUSTOMERS

sm@sureshmay.com

678-653-6610

How to Create Money Out of Thin Air
(FREE Video Training: $97 Value)

Before you dive into the deep blue seas of creating marketing campaigns that excite customers to buy from your business forever, pull out your phone right now and **text your name and email address to 276-565-7424 and follow the simple instructions to learn the secrets of the rich** that allow them to create wealth and income without an upfront investment.

This can be done easily- all you have to do is get the simple tricks that reveal how to see the opportunities right before your eyes.

The videos will come directly to your text messages- just click the text link and enjoy!

Again, **text your name and email address to 276-565-7424 and follow the simple instructions to learn how to create wealth out of thin air NOW!**

HOW TO CREATE LIFETIME CUSTOMERS

LEVERAGE *the* MARKETING POWER *of the* INTERNET *&* MOBILE TECHNOLOGY *to* QUICKLY GET NEW CUSTOMERS, HAVE THEM SPEND MORE MONEY, *&* KEEP THEM BUYING FOREVER

SURESH MAY
SURESHMAY.COM

JETTON GROUP PUBLISHING   ATLANTA

TO ALL STRUGGLING ENTREPRENEURS who came from nothing and started with only courage, will, and a big vision, this one is for you.

CONTENTS

SECTION 3: HOW TO MAKE CUSTOMERS BUY MORE FREQUENTLY

Preface

Can you *really* create lifetime customers?
Absolutely.

Of course you must treat customers fairly (and solve a huge problem that people are actively seeking a solution for), but creating lifetime customers can be easier than you think. And with Internet-enabled mobile technology powering our connections and social interactions, you can acquire customers *faster than at any other point in history.*

Whether you're a veteran entrepreneur or a rookie just starting out with digital marketing, you should have three major goals for your business:

1. Get a flood of new customers
2. Increase each customer's average order size
3. Make customers buy more frequently

That's it. Simple, right?

All marketing and business success boils down to these three goals, and this book has been crafted and designed with care to help you accomplish these goals quickly and easily!

Section One is all about acquiring those seemingly hard-to-get new customers. If you are having trouble generating fresh business or selling your current products and services, the four chapters in this section will show you how to get affluent customers buying your products faster than you ever thought possible.

Section Two reveals how to make buyers spend more money with ease. People love to buy a product or service if presented with the right offer, and the four chapters in this section will show you how to make people buy *everything* you sell!

Section Three gives the top secrets on how to keep customers buying more frequently and how to have them coming back forever. These four chapters will help give you constant business by leveraging tactics from phone companies and other industries that have stood the test of time.

The framework of this book allows you to read from cover to cover to build a profitable, customer-centric business from the ground up, *or* you can skip through to any chapter that covers your business's biggest issues.

The possibilities are endless, and you are only

limited by your imagination, dedication, and speed of implementation.

Ready to get started? I know I am! Follow along and I'll help you build the business of your dreams.

Suresh May
Atlanta, Georgia
July 15, 2014

Throughout the book, I'll share a few of my clients' stories. These clients are people who were having difficulty maximizing and capitalizing on the potential of their businesses. For the purpose of this book, and in an effort to respect personal and professional privacies, names, locations, and some circumstances have been dramatized.

Section 1:
How to Get a Flood of New Customers

ONE

How to Easily Get Customers Who Spend a Lot of Money

The golden rule for every business man is this: Put yourself in your customer's place.
– ORISON SWETT MARDEN

PUNTA CANA, DOMINICAN REPUBLIC

A YEAR AGO, BETHANY was inches away from death. Here she was again, staring death directly in the face. Except this time, she would put her life at stake with flair, and a lot more adrenaline-filled excitement.

"Jump! Jump! *Juuuuuuuuump!*" Bethany heard a voice give her the final command, but as the deafening, tornado-like winds slapped her in the face, she could only hear the sky-diving instructor's last words come through as a faint whisper.

As her feet balanced on the edge of the plane

12,500 feet over the cloud-covered world, she could feel her heart beating through her chest like a Questlove drum solo. She took a deep breath, closed her deep chestnut eyes, and leapt directly into the sun-kissed powder blue skies without a care in the world.

As she darted through the sky at 115 miles per hour, Bethany felt a powerful jerk when the parachute ejected from her backpack. She looked around the sky and saw Jamie, Sara, and Emily floating with her towards the luscious, green grasslands– all of them with grins bigger than *Alice in Wonderland's* Cheshire Cat– and all she could do was smile.

"That was amazing!" Emily screamed as her long, toned legs safely landed on Earth. "Oh my God, Bethany! Thank you for renting this island and inviting us all on this girls' retreat!" All of Bethany's friends cosigned the sentiment with excited laughs and big hugs.

"You're welcome, ladies! I'm just glad that my health and finances were good enough to go on vacation with you *and* sponsor the trip! Let's get out of these sky-diving suits so we can go shop for some sexy dresses for our night out on these gorgeous beaches," Bethany said with excitement and satisfaction.

For the first time in a long time, Bethany was elated.

Last year she couldn't even go on the all girls

retreat with her friends because she was stuck serving low-profit, high-headache customers in her wedding planning business, Once in a Lifetime Weddings.

She started the business from a place of love: Weddings made her heart sing, and there was nothing she enjoyed more than helping joyous brides-to-be plan the most romantic, idealistic day of their lives.

Bethany developed her passion for planning weddings from her mother, Anne, who made wedding dresses. When Bethany was a child, she and her mother looked through wedding magazines for hours on end, entranced by the masterfully crafted dresses.

Unfortunately, all of Bethany's love and fond memories soon changed: A few months after working with low-paying clients with small budgets, her adoration for the business vanished, and her feelings reappeared as horror.

Instead of helping brides create memorable weddings that no one would ever forget, she'd somehow only attracted clients who wanted lavish weddings on penny pinched budgets.

She was working 15 hour days, completely drained from stress, and like most people who have businesses that do not make enough money, she did not know how to get the high-paying customers she truly desired.

Everyday, she struggled to figure out where her

next client was coming from, if the client would be able to pay her, and if she would have the energy to provide the best possible service and experience. Bethany never let her frustrations show to her clientele, and she was always able to deliver a beautiful wedding, so she was often recommended by happy clients to even *more* couples with minuscule budgets.

Bethany was fed up, and she knew she had to make a drastic change. So she did.

* * *

If you have ever been like Bethany—worried about how you would get high paying clientele so you can stop chasing the broke ones—or if you have ever wondered how to get clients and customers to pay *exactly* what you are worth, then dive into the ocean of secrets that are uncovered within this chapter and learn exactly what Bethany did.

Your Most Important Business Breakthrough: Understand that You Are in the Marketing Business

This is easily the most important lesson in business, and that is why it comes first in this book: No matter what industry you are in– baked goods, retail, industrial supplies, software, real estate, or selling homemade copies of music and movies from your favorite artists and movie stars out of the trunk of your old beat up Buick Oldsmobile (which *is* illegal, but I can't knock the hustle), you are in the marketing business.

If you sell hamburgers for profit, it is very easy to think that you are in the burger or restaurant business– but the truth is, you are really in the business of selling and marketing burgers to consumers.

As an entrepreneur, your main responsibility is to get customers to buy your products and services. It is great to have the "best tasting" burger, but if you have eaten at any fast food restaurants lately, I would be willing to bet almost anything that your mother can make a burger better than those fast food chains.

The businesses that succeed understand that they are in the business of 1) knowing what the market wants, 2) targeting the subset of that market with disposable income, and 3) delivering the product the market wants.

In that order.

When I got started in business, I really screwed this up.

In the Summer of 2007, I got the bright idea to start a nutritional supplement company called Über Human Institute, LLC. I created a product called

ÜBERQUICK that helped athletes maximize their explosive power and speed. I played basketball in college, so I decided to target the amateur basketball market because I knew it very well. I understood our pains, aspirations, and I even had insider knowledge on the lingo that only players, coaches, and those closest to the game understood.

With a $6,000 investment from my lovely mother, I thought I had everything I needed to strike it rich QUICK!

Boy, was I wrong.

For fifteen plus years I lived in the basketball market, so I knew exactly what the market wanted, but I never had anyone teach me about targeting a market with disposable income. I grew up not having much, but I still overlooked the fact that the majority of this market did not have any disposable income.

Shortly after I got the product manufactured and shipped to my garage, I began running Facebook, Google, and niche magazine ads to begin marketing to these ball players, but the sales were trickling in like a slow-dripping faucet.

I was a novice businessman, so there were quite a few things that were off with my sales and marketing skills, but the largest and most important thing I missed the mark on was that I targeted people who did not have the cash to pay me.

When that happens, you will not make any money.

Sound familiar?

If it doesn't, awesome for you! But if you are like most other entrepreneurs, I'm sure it rings a bell.

You can have the best product on the market, but if you are targeting the wrong consumer, your product will never sell.

After a mentor taught me that I should target an active, older market that had money *and* athletic aspirations, my sales of ÜBERQUICK skyrocketed. I signed both an NFL and NBA player, and I had the #1 MMA fighters in the world use ÜBERQUICK to help maximize their explosive power and speed.

My fortune and the outcome of my first business changed because I finally understood that I was in the marketing business— and a part of that means understanding exactly *who* you need to target in order to reach your business and profit goals.

If you want customers who want to give you a ton of money, who are easy to sell to, who will not haggle you on price, and who won't stress you out, walk down the proverbial yellow brick road and follow these simple steps.

Step 1: Find a Smoking Hot Market

In sharp marketing circles, it is often said, "If everyone is your customer, then *no one* is your customer."

This is very sound marketing advice, and I would also add this: Just because you know intimate details of a market segment, does not mean that the market is qualified to do business with you, nor does your familiarity with a particular market mean you should target that market.

Researching your customers and your target market cannot be overstated. There are hundreds of thousands of businesses in the entrepreneurial graveyard because they never took the time to really understand *everything* about the person they wanted to sell their product or service to.

When you are in the early stages of market selection, it's impossible to do too much market research. To get you started on defining the ideal market to effectively sell your product or service, let's start with a few essential questions you need to answer:

1. Are there enough people in the market?

There are not any hard rules as to what size market you need.

Use the Google Keyword Tool to search common phrases and words that people in your market would use to find what you want to sell.

As a rule of thumb, make sure the keywords and phrases you plan to use to target your market's needs get more than 10,000 web searches per month.

If your research reveals that the keywords get more than 10,000 searches per month, this lets you know that a lot of people are actively searching for the solution to a problem that you can fulfill.

2. Is the market going to be big enough for you to enter and make a profit? Is the market dying, or is it constantly growing?

You may have heard a lot of self-proclaimed marketing "gurus" instruct you to "niche down" or "find a niche." Before now, you may have even believed them.

If you have swallowed those placebos in the past, forget that terrible advice moving forward.

The largest companies in the world look for MASS markets that are growing, and this is what you are going to do as well.

Find a growing market with a ton of active buyers in place, and I'll show you how to jump right in, add a ton of value, and position yourself to walk out of the bank with black duffel bags full of cash (legally)!

3. Is this market of people irrationally passionate?

Since you are reading this book, there is a strong chance that you are incredibly passionate about business, adding some kind of value to a marketplace, and making money to do whatever you like.

You probably have a bookshelf full of sales, marketing, leadership, and personal development books. You likely read the Forbes and Wall Street Journal, and spend your time on the internet listening to TED Talks.

If I've pegged you correctly, you are the kind of customer that I want to offer my products and services to. You have an insatiable appetite to learn more, do more, and be more when it's related to business, and I want to serve you by giving you exactly what you want, all while making a profit in the process. Everyone wins!

Rabid fans are everywhere: Some women have hundreds of pairs of shoes, sneakerheads stand outside of shoe stores for hours waiting on the new Jordans, and Apple fanboys wait days for the release of the new iPhone.

These fans go crazy for the objects of their desire, and they will spend their last dollar to get it. Your mission, should you choose to accept it, is to create something that a passionate market wants and get in the path of the monsoon flow of money.

4. Does your potential market have its own magazines?

If you are targeting a market that has a popular

niche magazine, that is a great sign of said market's profitability. If you want to get a magazine's readership and demographic information, go to its website and get its Rate Card.

The Rate Card will give you target market data such as income ranges, ages, gender, education level, and the number of subscriptions for the magazine.

If you are targeting a market that has a strong online magazine or blog presence, you can go to http://www.alexa.com and quickly browse that magazine or blog's URLs to get user data and learn about sites that cater to your target market.

5. Is this market qualified to do business with you?

This is EASILY the most important question when deciding which market you will target. Oftentimes, marketers and business owners will get so excited about an idea that they forget about (or they do not know) the importance of targeting a market segment that can pay you.

That sounded so ridiculous as I wrote it (who would invest in a market that cannot pay, right?), but you would be surprised at how many businesses fail simply because their target market segment cannot afford to pay the price for the solution the business is offering.

There are three things that a market needs to

have for it to be totally qualified to do business with you, and we call this the Lifetime Customer Profit Trifecta:

First, make sure that it has the willingness to buy. This means that the market wants to buy what you are selling. Period.

Second, be certain that it has the ability to buy. This means the people in the market have disposable income and/or a credit card so they can afford what you are offering. People who do not have much disposable income usually have to make either/or buying choices, so this is more likely to kill the impulse buy and increase your refund rate.

Third, make sure your market is affordably reachable. This means that you are able to reach people with your current marketing budget no matter what media your target market is in. There are fixed costs to get new customers, so if you need to run $100,000 magazine ads with the goal of getting new leads, make sure you can afford the price to profitably generate these leads and sales.

6. Does the market have its own jargon or language?

Can you identify slang or market-specific terms that your target market uses exclusively?

Let's say you want to target the amateur basketball market—which I highly advise against because amateur athletes typically do not have any disposable income. Ballplayers say emphatic phrases such as "AND ONE!" when they score a basket and get fouled at the same time.

The phrase is so popular among the basketball market that an entire street basketball league was created and named after it. Basketball players also use expressions like "mouse in the house", which means you have a smaller guy guarding you when you are in the paint. Even "paint" is basketball slang for the painted free throw area!

You can learn these things by talking to the people in your target market. Listen to what they say. Read their blogs and watch how they communicate with each other– what you learn could be the difference between a losing and profitable marketing campaign.

7. Does your potential target market have its own conferences and events?

Depending on the event, people spend hundreds and even thousands of dollars attending conferences. A ticket to a blowout event may cost $1,000 and up, but the expenses do not stop there: there will be airfare, hotel fees, food, a rental car, and entertainment.

When people in your target market frequently hold conferences, that is a sure-fire way to let you know that they have the disposable income needed for you to make a profit.

8. Can you find a direct competitor?

A lot of entrepreneurs and business owners try to get into businesses where they do not have any competition. If you have not learned by now, this is a terrible idea.

It is not a good sign if there is no competition because it usually means that there is not any money being made in that market. Look for another business who is selling something very similar to what you are selling and make a more appealing offer.

9. Can you find five other products that are being sold to your target market? How much are advertisers paying to advertise to this market?

When you are looking for five other products, search for related, complementary products. For instance, if you're selling a book about golfing, you would look for people selling golf shoes, golf clubs, golf shirts, etc.

Clearly you can find these things in the golf market. This lets you know that a lot of marketers are playing in this market, and that should tell you that there is a bunch of money to be made in this massive niche.

If you notice marketers spending a lot of money to acquire leads and capture customers, this reveals that those customers are highly profitable.

This is great news because after I teach you how to properly set up a back-end business model in Section 2, How to Make Buyers Spend More Money, the customers of those complementary businesses will be highly profitable for you.

10. Does your market have its own celebrities?

Can you identify people who everyone in the market looks up to? Can you identify people who everyone wants to be like?

If you can, your business and your profits can skyrocket by leveraging the association with these local, international, or market-specific celebrities. In Chapter 9, I'll teach you how to become a celebrity and dominate your market.

Step 2: Create a Customer Avatar

After you have done all of the heavy lifting identifying your market, you need to create a customer avatar. You may be asking, "What's a customer avatar?"

To keep it simple, a customer avatar is a profile or an outline of your ideal customer.

As a marketer of goods, you must to do your best to know *absolutely everything* you can about the people in your target market.

If you are targeting single, Caucasian women

who are between the ages of 40 and 50, know what kind of homes they live in, what kind of cars they drive, their zip codes, if they have dogs, if they have kids, etc.

Ask yourself questions like: Have they ever been married? What are their husbands like? Are they divorced? Have they been divorced more than once? What are their buying habits? Do they smoke or drink?

When you are crafting your ads (Chapter 3) and your sales messages (Chapter 4), being specific and as relevant as possible will increase your sales. If you can make people say to themselves "Oh wow! They are talking directly to me!", you'll be able to more effectively sell your products and services because you understood and conveyed intimate details of their lives.

Create a customer avatar that leaves no stones unturned. Study the person that you wish to sell to, and your customers will have no choice but to pay you well.

Step 3: Go for the Money

Here is a HUGE myth-buster that should excite you: It is easier to sell to wealthy people than it is to sell to people with little to no money.

Many entrepreneurs think that it is easier to sell to people with little money because they think the rich elite have different mentalities when it comes to buying, and therefore amateur marketers think it will be harder to sell to rich, affluent markets.

This is simply not true.

Not only do rich and poor people share one of the six core buying motives (Desire for Gain, Fear of Loss, Comfort and Convenience, Security and Protection, Pride of Ownership, and Satisfaction of Emotion), rich people spend money more freely because it is easier for them to make buying decisions.

When low-income people make buying decisions, it usually comes down to sacrificing one thing or the other to make a purchase. If people in your target audience are on a tight budget, they have to make tough money decisions about what they are going to take from another aspect of their lives. This can kill your sales conversions because some people cannot afford what you are selling so they may never buy.

When rich people make a buying decision, they can buy whatever they want without having to make a financial sacrifice in another aspect of their lives.

Additionally, when you sell to the rich, you can sell your products and services at a higher price because high prices are associated with high quality and exclusivity.

Think about it: Why do you think people buy expensive homes, cars, and clothes? It's all because of the perception it creates. As a smart marketer, you should do your best to price your products high to capitalize off of your target audience's natural aspirational buying motives and tendencies.

If you don't learn anything else in this book, learn this, and learn it well: Always follow the money.

Step 4: Give People What They Want

One of the fastest ways to create wealth is to get in front of people who are ready to buy what you are selling.

Gary Halbert, one of the greatest copywriters who ever lived, tells a story about speaking to a crowd at one of his seminars. He asks the crowd a simple question: "If we all started a restaurant to compete against one another, and you could have one big advantage over every other restaurant, what would your big advantage be?"

The replies people shouted ranged from "A great location!" to "The best food!"

Gary said softly, "I'll give every one of you everything you asked for, and I will still put all of you out of business with my one thing."

Everyone in the crowd paused with anticipation.

Gary continued, "Give me a starving crowd."

If you sell to people who have a massive desire for your product or service, you can create wealth faster than you thought possible.

Oftentimes, when entrepreneurs and business owners go into business or develop new products, they start by developing an "awesome" product or service that they have created.

You may have experienced this: You've come up with what you think is a killer idea. You invest your time, energy, and money into creating it, and *POOF*! You are making zero dollars as fast as possible because no one buys it.

A better way to design products is to start with the desires of the market that you want to sell to, and then create a product or service that the market tells you it wants. This piece of marketing advice is easily worth the price of this book, and just so it'll sink in, I'll illustrate it with a story.

When I started out in my supplement business, I thought about what I wanted to create. I wanted the product to work, I wanted the bottle to have great packaging, and I wanted it to make a lot of money.

I thought so much about what I wanted and how great it would be, that I assumed the market would want it and think it was great as well.

That was the problem: I was so caught up in *what I wanted* to do that I did not stop and consider *what the market was demanding*.

When you start building a business thinking of what *you* want to create and sell, versus creating what *the market* says it wants, you will find yourself creating products that you are trying to push on the market.

To avoid this, you should poll the market, figure out what it wants, and then create *that*. This seems so simple, but I still find that a lot of entrepreneurs and business owners do not do it.

Sometimes, you may hit the business lottery by being successful in creating something you want to create without asking the market what it wants, but the odds are against you. If you want to guarantee the success of your business, find a starving crowd, ask the market what it wants, and create a product or service around it.

Knowing Who Your Real Buyer Is

Let's say you find a starving crowd of kids that are in a buying frenzy over a product that you want to sell. These kids are going crazy for it, so you begin a Facebook or Google AdWords campaign that targets this demographic.

You write your ad copy, create your landing pages for lead generation and sales, set your budgets, get the associated keywords, and press play on your ads. After a few days, you notice that sales are only trickling in, if at all.

What happened? What went wrong?

Assuming your campaign is set up correctly, you are likely targeting the wrong buyer. Since you're selling a product that targets children, you should be targeting their parents. But why?

Think about it. When you were a kid, who

bought everything for you? Your parent(s) or guardian(s). In our story, *the child is the end user,* but *the parent is the buyer.*

What does this mean? If your target market is dominated by kids, oftentimes they will not have credit cards or bank accounts, let alone two nickels to rub together. Even if you can sell them something, usually it is a harder sell because you have to sell them *and* their parents.The children don't have any money, so they cannot make buying decisions.

When you are crafting marketing messages to target the buyers (the parents), you want to write your message in a way that illustrates the benefits that your product or service will have on the kids, but write it so that those benefits speak to the parents' ultimate needs and desires for their kids' advancement.

For example, let's say the kids are going crazy over a brand new pair of roller skates. Since we know that we need to persuade parents into making and justifying a buying decision, we may talk about how the roller skates will give their kids a fun way to exercise and stay in shape or build relationships and social skills by interacting with other kids in their communities.

These are things all parents want for their kids. When you emphasize this value in your sales message, you will be more likely to sell more roller skates because the parent is the buyer.

Write ads that get the kids excited, but also be sure to understand who is making the buying decision so that you can satisfy those desires as well.

* * *

After Bethany took massive, guided action, Once in a Lifetime Weddings grew by 1271%, and netted $1,123,456.31 in profits in 312 days.

She is now working less.

She only spends time with the clients she chooses to work with, and she gets to fund exotic trips around the world with her friends and family.

As Bethany and her friends walked away from the grassy landing spot to get ready for their night on the town, she looked back at the golden water reflecting the setting sun. Bethany looked up to the sky and thought to herself with a grin, "Life *is* good."

* * *

Now that you have learned how to identify affluent customers who want to spend a lot of money, I am going to show you how to get an unlimited amount of wealthy prospects in your marketing funnel–all without cold prospecting.

Massive Action List

1. Write your customer avatar.

Think about the people you want to buy your product and service.

Where do they live? What do they like to do in their spare time? What kind of cars do they drive? Are they married? Are they single? Do they smoke? Do they drink? Do they have dogs? Do they have kids? What are their lifestyles like? What are their days like? Are they entrepreneurs? Do they wake up and go to work?

You need to understand every single thing you can about your market. After you take the time to learn about your ideal customer, you will write better sales messages and ads, which is essentially the key to helping you sell more products and services than your competition.

2. Answer the top ten questions in "Step 1: Find a Smoking Hot Market".

Answering these tough questions will help you decide if you should invest any time, energy, or money into your potential market.

Do not skim over this– lots of businesses are killed because they fail to take advantage of the power of targeting the right customer, and I do not want you to be the next victim.

If you want a full list of the most important customer avatar questions you need to ask to master your market, text your name and email address to 276-565-RICH(7424) or go to www.sureshmay.com/CLCgifts and get it for free!

TWO

How to Get Unlimited Leads Without Cold Prospecting

Doing business without advertising is like winking at a girl in the dark. You know what you are doing, but nobody else does.
- STUART H BRITT

SAN DIEGO, CA

IT WAS ALREADY the longest day possible, and since the brutal rejection was taking an Ultimate Fighting Championship-styled pounding on Josh's ego, it would not get better anytime soon.

Palms sweaty and heart racing, Josh picked up the phone to dial another cold prospect. He hated it, but he had to do it. It was the only way he knew how to get new leads.

"Hello, my name is Josh Lewis, and I'm with Burke Technologies. I'm calling today because I'd like to talk to you about..."

CLICK!!!

"Damn! That was the seventh hang up in a row," Josh said to himself. A blind man could see his immense discouragement. Josh was one of the company's top performers, but his pipeline was almost empty, and the entire office knew he was slumping for 29 days straight.

Henry, the CEO of Burke Technologies, saw the disappointed look on Josh's face. Henry had faced many sales slumps in his 27-year tenure, so he knew the look very well. Henry looked in Josh's direction and smiled. "Hey Josh, what's going on?"

"I'm having trouble getting decision makers on the phone," Josh said nervously.

Henry was the boss, and Josh knew Henry did not do well with underachievers.

Josh continued, "When I do get someone, they are usually disinterested, and the sales tactics that I usually use seem to be less and less effective."

Luckily for Josh, Henry was having a great Monday morning. He recently left the *Lifetime Customer Blueprint* marketing program in Atlanta, Georgia, and he had the solution to revive his downward sales.

"Don't worry Josh, you're one of my top performers, and our entire sales team is down this quarter," Henry said with a relaxed tone.

Josh was not used to seeing this side of Henry, especially when someone shared bad news with the type-A CEO.

"I have a solution," Henry continued. "This past weekend I learned some killer lead generation and sales tactics that will get us a flood of new, warm, pre-qualified leads without doing anymore cold calls. I'm excited for the office to implement these strategies, and I know you're going to crush it!"

Josh was surprised. Not only did he not get chewed out about his 29-day slump, his boss offered him a solution to solve every sales professional's biggest problem.

Josh replied, "Wow! I'm excited to hear about it! When can we get started?"

* * *

Never Make a Cold Call Again

If you have spent any amount of time doing manual sales like I have, you know that cold prospecting sucks. It doesn't matter if you are cold calling, cold emailing, or wearing out the soles of your shoes going door to door, cold sales are as painful as stubbing a toe. No matter how many times you do it, it is always unpleasant.

Not only does cold selling suck, but it is a huge waste of time in selling. Most star sales professionals spend most of their time talking to cold, dead leads, and this is hurting sales in every business in the world. Even if you separate prospecting from selling and closing deals, you will still have a business development representative talking to more unqualified prospects than qualified ones.

How fast do you think your business would multiply if you could only talk to warm, pre-qualified leads?

The Best Way to Get New Leads: Inbound vs Outbound Marketing

Before I reveal the solution, please do not get me wrong—because cold calling is excruciating does not mean that it never works—cold calling has built many businesses, but when you start talking about levels of effectiveness, it is definitely at the very bottom of the totem pole.

You may be asking yourself, "If you have a product or service, how can you consistently and effectively prospect new leads if you don't do it cold?"

The answer is simple: direct response marketing.

If cold selling is like a stranger interrupting your peaceful dinner (outbound marketing), then direct response is like having your best friend invite you to eat a delicious meal at your favorite restaurant (inbound marketing).

Direct response marketing is the art of making irresistible offers to your target audience that elicit a response or action directly from your target consumer.

One of the biggest reasons you should add direct response to your marketing arsenal to replace cold calling is because it gives you the power to create a flood of warm prospects who WANT to hear from you.

Here is how direct response marketing works: You make a valuable offer to a prospect that gets them into the beginning of your marketing funnel. You make this offer so irresistible and easy to take that it effortlessly creates a hot lead.

Once you have people raising their hands saying, "Hey, I'm interested in this kind of information," you have their permission to continue offering them value and to make your sales offer. After you take the time to get them to give you permission to market and sell to them, you will instantly have a more valuable prospect. Contrast that with calling someone who does not want to hear from you, and you can quickly see how valuable getting inbound leads will be to your business.

Another powerful benefit of using direct response marketing is that it can be integrated with other marketing mediums. For instance, let's say you are implementing a mobile marketing strategy and you need to figure out how to get customers to take action and respond to your offers.

You could do what most business owners do and post things like "Hey everyone! We're in business!" or, "Go to our website and check out our stuff!"

When you try to sell this way, it's ineffective

because people do not care about you or your business.

You may hope they do, but people only care about how you and your business can serve them. To solve this problem, make sure you post clear, benefit-driven, direct response styled offers in your internet and mobile marketing strategies.

I know you can visualize the value that direct response marketing will add to your arsenal, so let's get into the three most profitable ways to make offers that will create a stampede of affluent customers to your business.

How to Craft Irresistible Offers & Find the Hot Buyers

An offer can be anything- you can give something away for free, you can charge a dollar, you can make your product buy one, get one, and you can even legally rob people by overcharging them 100x the normal price.

Whatever pricing and offer strategy you use to get new leads and buyers, it will fall into one of the three major offer categories.

Before we get started, I must tell you that neither one of these offer styles are better or worse than any of the others. The one you choose should depend solely on your marketing goals and how qualified you want your warm, inbound leads.

Free Offers

If you have turned on a television in the last 50 years or surfed the internet in the last few seconds, you have without a doubt witnessed the free offer.

If done correctly, the goal of the free offer is simple: The merchant gives the prospect something valuable for free, and the prospect gives the merchant some kind of lead generating information in exchange.

When you give things away for free, naturally you're going to get the maximum amount of leads compared to the other two offer styles.

Having a bunch of fresh, new inbound leads is always awesome, but free offers usually attract the least qualified leads. This happens because free offers tend to get a lot of people who only want the free thing, and they may never have any intentions of actually buying your core offer.

In fact, using the criteria in Chapter 1, they may not even fit our profile of a qualified targeted prospect, and we shouldn't even be selling to them.

For example, think about the last time you followed your nose to a mall food court. It doesn't matter what time of day it is, every time you go you will see people holding up free food samples.

Now, if you give me some free food, I'm eating it! Even though a lot of folks will get a free taste, you will get a lot of people who will eat the free sample but have zero intentions of making a purchase.

On the opposite end of the spectrum, you will get some people who will say, "Oh wow, this food is tasty! I think I'll buy this!"

That's the power of a free offer. Sometimes you can offer someone so much value for free that they'll want to buy the product that you plan to sell them.

If you are asking, "Why does this work?", that's a great question.

Here is the psychology behind it: When you give someone something for free, you implement the Law of Reciprocity. The Law of Reciprocity states that if you do something for someone, they naturally want to do something for you.

Have you ever asked a friend for a favor? Of course you have. After your friend delivers the favor (assuming you're not a mooch), you naturally want to do something for that friend in return. Returning generosity has a high value in society, and for that reason, most people like to "pay back" acts of giving and kindness.

As a marketer, the Law of Reciprocity gives you huge power because the exchange doesn't always have to be of equal value.

In our mall food court example, just because a merchant gives you a free piece of chicken, clearly you're not going to give them a free piece of chicken back. The reciprocity from customers will be their money, and that's enough to tip the scale in the merchant's favor.

When qualified prospects take you up on your free offer, you can capitalize off of another psychological law: Commitment and Consistency.

People have an obsessive desire to appear consistent with what we've already done. Once we've made a choice or taken a stand, we feel personal and interpersonal pressures to behave congruently with that commitment. These internal and external pressures make us continue down a path that justifies our earlier decision.

Think about a time when you were having a debate with someone. If the person you are speaking with takes a strong stance on a particular point, it does not matter if they are right or wrong, you can bet anything that they will do their best to stand firm in their position.

Even if you call them out on it, usually they will stick with their decision even if they know they are wrong. It's totally ridiculous, but from a societal view, it does not pay to look like an inconsistent person.

How can you apply this to your business?

When you get someone to opt into your list for something free, and then you make another paid offer related to what they just received, oftentimes they will make a purchase just to remain consistent with their previous decision to get your free thing. When you do this correctly, leads who come to you through a free offer can quickly become very profitable buyers.

Another excellent reason to offer things for free is because it totally removes the risk from your prospects. We all hate making bad buying decisions, and when you offer something for free, you remove the potential risk of people looking stupid for making that purchase. When you are selling products and services on the internet and mobile devices, people are naturally more apprehensive because of digital fraud.

You can have an excellent product that solves a huge problem in the marketplace, but your prospects may not buy from you because they don't want to feel dumb, used, or hoodwinked out of their hard-earned money.

Always keep the wariness of your prospects in mind. When you are implementing offers, do your best to understand the psychological tricks that your prospects' minds will play on them, and add risk reversal copy elements (you will learn this in Chapter 4) that will ensure they purchase with confidence.

With all this talk about getting hot leads by giving stuff away, you may think it's OK to say, "Hey everyone! Come grab this widget for FREE!"

Stop it. That's not even close to cool.

In order for a free offer to work, it's important for you to tell, show, and prove why the value is over zero dollars. You have to make the prospect believe that the offer is worth something.

You can easily achieve this by adding a price value to the free offer, and you can emphasize that other people have paid for the offer. You don't want to just give away something that is perceived as cheap or free for everyone. The offer has to have some kind of value to your target market, and you have to prove that value. When you see marketing copy that reads "This $29 offer is free for a limited time," the marketer makes you think you are getting something that has a true marketplace value.

Do you remember when I told you that you can make a profit by having free front-end offers? If you want to implement this strategy, make sure you have your back-end marketing funnel (Chapter 7) set up properly in order to profit from your free front-end offers.

If you have ever wondered, "How are these businesses making money giving things away for free or at a deep discount?"

Savvy businesses still profit because they have a back-end marketing funnel that capitalizes off of them breaking even or taking a small loss on the front-end.

Qualifying and One Time Offers

The second offer type is a low-priced qualifying or one-time offer. This may be a $1 trial offer, a free plus shipping offer, or any other offer where the prospect makes a small investment in the first or second step of your marketing funnel.

Qualifying offers are designed specifically to find out who is willing to become a buyer. If a business runs a free plus shipping promotion, they are building a database of paying customers in order to sell them a more expensive product or service.

Let's say a marketer is offering a DVD valued at $50, and they say you can get it for free if you pay the shipping price. The reason a marketer would do that is because they want to see who's willing to pull out a credit card and buy something. After you make the free purchase, the marketer will take you through a series of upsells with the goal of making a profit. Even if you're selling software with a $1 trial, the same concept applies.

If anyone could make a lead generation argument against low-priced qualifying offers, it would be that you will normally acquire a lot less leads than a free offer.

This is a small draw back, and the upside is that you will build a list of buyers—and that is infinitely more powerful than a list of free subscribers. If you want to get fancy with this, you can implement a 2-step front-end offer: Make your first step lead magnet a totally free item, and make your second step a low-priced offer.

This can be the best of both worlds because it allows you to separate your buyers from your subscribers.

Full-Price Offer

The third offer type is a full-priced offer. Full-price offers can be great, but when you make full-price offers, you are only going to get people who are ready to buy *now*.

If a prospect takes your full-price offer, naturally he or she is the most qualified buyer, but by offering the full-priced version first, you're going to miss a lot of leads who are on the fence about making a purchase.

Full-priced offers are great once you have added value to your list and you have nurtured relationships, but as a front-end offer for new business, it's better to offer some sort of free information to get prospects to make a small commitment.

Digital Ad Fundamentals: Sell the Click, Not the Product

As digital marketers, we want to focus our marketing efforts on gaining responses from prospects. You will often see marketers using branding style ads or ads that attempt to get the order directly from the ad.

Smart marketers focus on selling the clicks instead of attempting to sell the main product. What does this mean?

If you're running an ad for a course on how to

golf better, you want to get people to click on your ad based on their minds' most dominant desires. I recently started playing golf, and time and time again I hear a lot of guys trying to improve the yards they get on their drive.

If I wanted to market to these golfers, in my ads I may say, "Get the top secret to add 100 yards to your drive! Click here now!" If a golfer who wants to improve his drive sees that ad, he is going to click.

Compare that with an ad that says, "Buy this new golf club! Click here now!" Even if the golf club will add 100 yards to their drive, there is not a clear benefit to click on the ad to see the offer, and the people reading the ad are going to ask themselves, "What is that going to help me do?"

Another way to get prospects to click on your ads and come into your marketing funnel is to use education-based marketing. The most valuable commodity is information, and in one way or another, that's what we're all looking for.

Using the golf example, you may advertise information that says, "Learn the top pro secrets Tiger Woods used to win his PGA tournaments. These secrets will also help you increase your swing by 221 yards!"

As long as the education is based on information your target market wants, it will make them interested in going to your site and getting into your marketing funnel.

How to Create a Website that Prints Money

What do you do when your prospect clicks your ad and comes to your site? What do you offer to capture the lead?

There is a lot of confusion around this topic. A lot of business owners I consult start off with brochure or "business card" style websites. We have all seen these: there is a "home" page, an "about" page, a "contact" page, and maybe even a "product" page. If business owners think highly of themselves, they may have pretty pictures or even music. These sites may be beautiful, but if you are not capturing leads and making offers, these pages will not help you make any money online or on mobile devices.

Some of my clients who have a better clue begin with ecommerce-style sites. These site styles offer products for sale so they do a better job of selling than brochure style sites, but if you want to have the most effective selling site, you need to have some sort of direct response element to your web presence.

I know you want to make as much money as you can, so your single goal should be to capture leads and sell products. A direct response style site will give you the ability to do this. You will need separate landing pages for separate products. You are going to make offers to get your client's name, email address, or whatever contact information you want to help you follow-up with your prospects.

Whatever information you want to collect, your single focus is to capture leads and build your market share, add them in your marketing funnel, nurture the lead, control the follow-up process, and make the sale in the near future.

The Most Valuable Part of Your Business

This is easily the most important section in this chapter. After you sell the click in your ad and take the prospect to an irresistible offer to capture the lead, you begin building the most valuable asset in your business: a customer list.

Building a list of leads and buyers is the best solution to creating lifetime cash flow and wealth in your business. A list is commonly called your "fan base" or your "following". Whatever you decide to call it, you need to start creating one ASAP.

To illustrate an example of the power of list building, I think about the Grammy award-winning singer and superstar Beyoncé Knowles.

When she launched her album, Beyoncé, in 2013, she launched it in the middle of the night on Instagram with a 15-second video. She didn't have any big music business promotion, but her album went platinum almost *immediately.*

How did this happen? She had a huge "list" or fan base. This may not be exciting to you, but it gets me going because it tells me that I can build up a group of people who are interested in my message, product, or my service and I can market to them whenever I want to.

When you can go platinum (or sell a bunch of product) with the aid of only a 15-second video, that's massive power. Most businesses don't take the time to build up a list of devoted fans they can re-market to on their own terms– and that's a huge mistake.

So how do you build a list?

One of easiest and fastest ways to build a list is by offering information to a group of interested people as a lead magnet.

In the Beyoncé example, she could use a new song as a lead magnet. It is as simple as her saying, "Hey guys, I'm going to give you a free song on my website. Go to beyonce.com and check it out!"

This would instantly drive traffic back to her website. After you get to her site, she should have an opt-in form to collect whatever information she thinks she needs to keep in touch with her market before they can listen to her free song.

After she builds her list, she can then market an album to a qualified group of people who are primed to buy! Capitalizing off a list is as simple as that.

Once you spend the time to build your list, DO NOT ignore the people on it or allow them to forget about you. You have to keep adding value and nurturing your list. A lot of people who build lists don't follow up with them, leading the prospect list to become unresponsive.

You have invested a lot of time and money to build this database, so it would behoove you to constantly send your list valuable information relative to your market.

How often you mail your list is up to you, but you want to consistently communicate with your contacts. The content you send can be in the form of video, audio, PDF, or any other format you can think of.

Whatever you send, just make sure it's enormously valuable to the list. If we again use the Beyoncé example, she could send snippets of songs, new video releases, or backstage footage of her at a concert. If you love Beyoncé, you'll love this kind of content and it would be enormously valuable to you.

This is very simple to replicate. All you have to do is put together awesome lead generating content for your business.

* * *

Remember Josh and his cold calling blues? Eight months after Henry taught his team the fundamentals he learned in the *Lifetime Customer*

Blueprint marketing program, everyone, including Josh, was breaking sales records.

Burke Technologies went from doing $2.1 million in yearly sales, to being on pace to close out the 4th quarter with close to $1 million dollars in monthly billings. All of this happened because their sales reps stopped wasting their time chasing cold, unproductive leads.

Now is the time to experience the power of warm leads flooding your business like a tsunami!

Massive Action List

1. Brainstorm different offers you can make to get people into your marketing funnel.

Think about what you sell, and think about what's on your target prospect's mind. What do you offer? What kind of information would be valuable to your audience? Think about what you can give away to generate warm inbound leads for your business to eliminate your reliance on cold prospecting.

2. Build your customer list!

Add forms to your site to collect customer names and email addresses. This is the most important thing you can do to build wealth in your business.

If you want a full list of the most effective ways to generate warm leads and build your list, go to www.sureshmay.com/CLCgifts or text your name and email address to 276-565-RICH(7424) and get it for free!

THREE

How To Write Money-Making Advertisements

The spider looks for a merchant who doesn't advertise so he can spin a web across his door and lead a life of undisturbed peace!
– MARK TWAIN

WASHINGTON, DC

S HE WAS BURNING money as fast as bad gamblers lose mortgage payments at a casino.

"My ads are terrible, and I'm losing almost $2,000 *every day*! I have no idea where people are coming from or what they are doing on my site!" Claire spoke with a sad, concerned look. "I've been using Google AdWords and Facebook Ads for months, but I haven't converted anyone into customers. What could I possibly be doing wrong?"

"It sounds like quite a bit," I replied calmly. "I could break down your entire marketing funnel, but for starters, your headlines need to be benefit-driven, and it will help if you send every segment of your market to a different, specific landing page."

As I slammed my last domino down on the table to win the game, I looked into Claire's clear, blue eyes. Her worry was evident. I'd just met Claire an hour ago, but like most people do after they have a few cocktails, she told me her entire life story.

For the past eight years, Claire owned a chain of successful specialty fitness studios, and her sales grow every year. Just like most ambitious business owners, she wanted to expand her business by marketing online.

The profits from her business gave her a huge marketing budget, so Claire spent her money on branding style ads that did not illicit a response from her target consumer. She was essentially throwing cash at the issue, and she needed an army of help.

Claire's eyes widened before she spoke. "So I should not create one ad that targets everyone?"

I replied, "Not if you want to stop bleeding money. Ads that target everyone usually speak to no one, and that's the main reason people aren't opting in and taking action."

With a look of confusion, Claire replied, "Why do I have to have a different landing page for every market segment?"

"Every segment has different needs, and those

needs should be addressed individually. If you're trying to sell a weight loss pill to men and women, you need to understand that they likely have different end desires for using it. A man may want to get ripped, but a woman may want to lose belly fat and tone her arms." I paused to let the point sink in. "At a minimum, you should have two different ads and two different pages that target both of these market segments."

Claire smiled, took another sip, and she finally asked the million dollar question. "I understand now. That makes a ton of sense, Suresh. Now that I know I should be specific with my targeting, how do I write ads that make money?"

I grinned and said, "I thought you'd never ask."

* * *

The Most Profitable Part of Your Ad

In the world of ad writing, some of the greatest ad men and women alive would argue that the headline is the most important component of your ad. A headline is your ad's brain. Just as your body won't function without your brain, your ad won't work without a killer headline. People won't read past a boring, drab headline, and if you miss this mark, it will render your remaining content useless.

Powerful marketing sentences start with the

result your customer wants. If you are using a direct response style advertisement, the headline will be the first thing your target customer sees. Your headline should be so captivating that it stops your target customers in their tracks. It should be specific to their desires, and it should make them want to read the next line in your ad.

Beginning with your headline, every sentence you write should be so engaging that it pulls your reader to the next line, like the fragrance of a delicious, home-cooked breakfast wakes you from your sleep and pulls you into your mother's kitchen.

Five Important Qualities of Great Headlines

The path of profitable copywriting is a long, winding road, so let's take the first steps and discover the five major qualities of excellent headlines.

1. Self-Interest or Benefit-Driven Quality

The most important of the five qualities is having a self-interest or a benefit-driven aspect to your headline. I'm addicted to studying all kinds of ads, and the most common mistake I see businesses make is talking about how great THEY think their businesses are versus how this greatness translates into helping the customer.

For example, if you have a lawn care company and you created the "World's Best Lawn Seed," most businesses will say "We have the greatest lawn seed in the world!" in their advertising.

A better way to market is to think about the people who are going to buy your lawn seed, and how the seed will benefit them. What do they want? What's the end result they seek?

Naturally, they want a beautiful lawn. I am sure you or someone you know has a gorgeous, green lawn that is kept masterfully manicured. The lawn is always being cut, trimmed, and conditioned to maintain its beauty. When someone rolls by a house with an exquisite lawn, one can't help but to admire it.

As a lawn seed business, if you want your lawn seed to be successful, your ads should speak to your market's desires with phrases such as: "You can have the best lawn in the neighborhood," or "You can get the most beautiful, green, and full lawn imaginable."

These are the end results that people interested in lawn seeds want. You want to avoid advertising *what you think* about your lawn seed. You do not want to advertise how great it is, you want to talk about how it's going to benefit the person who is buying it.

You have to tap into your prospect's mind and

capture those wants in your headline.

2. Inclusion and Exclusion

The second excellent feature of a headline is its ability to include the people you want reading your ads and exclude the people you don't want reading your ads.

If you use the headline "Five Days to Remove Corns Guaranteed" to a target group of people who have big corns on their feet, you'll get a lot of people to take action.

If people without corns read this same headline, they are not going to be interested in your ad, and that's exactly what you want because they aren't the target prospect.

If readers have corns bursting through their shoes as they read that headline, they're going to consume the ad because you're talking about solving one of their direct problems.

When you do a great job of leveraging inclusion and exclusion in your copy, you'll quickly experience a boost in qualified warm leads and sales.

3. Tell Them Something New

News sells. Anytime something new happens–whether it's breaking news or a young kid doing something cool in school–the news gets our attention and it makes us react. People love to talk, they adore gossip, and they live to talk about what's new in the media.

If there's something new and exciting about your product or if your product is related to something that's going on in the news, use it in your headline because you'll pick up a lot of your target audience that way.

4. Tap into Their Curiosity

People take action when they are curious, but use this quality wisely. Curiosity alone may not be effective enough for you to pull your target audience, but when combined with a news or self interest quality, curiosity is an excellent way to increase the pulling power of your headline.

5. Make it Quick and Easy, but Be Believable

Let's face it: We live in a microwave society. Most people want things quick and easy, so this has become a huge selling point. If people can get a quick result from using your product or service, drive that point home. A lot of ads overdo quick and easy to the point where it becomes unbelievable, so sell your solution in a way that people can believe your claim enough to take action.

Speaking of believability, specifics always trump general information. When you're talking about numbers, figures, or percentages, be as specific as possible because it's more persuasive.

If I told you "89 people" took my offer versus saying "almost 100," the specificity of 89 seems more authentic, and it will naturally breed more sales.

Bonus: Avoid Negative Headlines

I'll keep it simple: Try your best to avoid negative headlines. You want to offer your prospects cheerful, positive headlines that put people in a good mood and a positive spirit.

Mass Market Advertising = Maximum Cash

When you begin your advertising journey online, you'll hear a lot of conflicting advice. In many marketing circles, you'll hear people say, "Find a small niche market to sell your products and services." Contrary to popular belief, I think this is some of the worst advice a business owner can get.

When you begin marketing a product or service, place yourself in a position to make the maximum amount of money as quickly as possible in a growing market.

While you can make a lot of money in the niches, niche markets are usually sub-groups of mass markets. Mass markets are where the massive amounts of wealth are, and all you need are two notable examples from superstar entrepreneurs to make the point clear: Bill Gates with Microsoft and Ted Turner with Turner Broadcasting.

When Microsoft was introduced to the marketplace, the goal and vision was simple: Get the Windows operating system on every computer in the world. Although Microsoft was in the personal computer market, it created a product that everyone in the world could use. Regardless of our individual end goals, operating systems made computers easier for the end user, and that resulted in a multi-billion dollar business.

Ted Turner had a similar vision with Turner Broadcasting: Everyone wants to be entertained. From sports and reality TV to everything in between, just about everyone has watched television. Creating a cable network is a mass market vision, and the results yield sales in the billions.

If you decide to advertise to a sub-niche market, you're naturally going to have a smaller reach and you'll make less money. There isn't anything wrong with going for a sub-niche market, but I teach my clients to go for the bigger markets so they can have a greater impact and make more money.

Find the Biggest Reasons People Buy

The best way to guarantee that you write money-making ads is to understand the most desirable consumer appeal.

An appeal is simply the most dominant reason why your reader will make a buying decision. Your job is to lead with the broadest, most powerful appeal that market research reveals, then apply your product or service to that dominant desire.

Speaking of desire, every mass human desire, no matter who you are or where you are from, has three dimensions. These dimensions dictate how well your product or service will sell.

Dimension 1: Urgency, Intensity, and Degree of Demand

The first dimension of mass desire is urgency, intensity, and degree of demand to be satisfied. For example, if you have arthritis, you want to get rid of arthritic pain as quickly as possible.

Contrast that with having a minor headache– you would want to get rid of it, but it's not nearly as painful as the sometimes crippling effect of arthritis. When you think about what you want to sell to your consumer, make sure the problem you're solving is strong enough that it has an urgent need to be fixed. If you plan this well, your prospect will respond to your ads as if you were giving away money.

Dimension 2: Degree of Repetition and Staying Power

The second dimension you should cover is the staying power and degree of repetition, or the inability of your prospect's problem to become easily satisfied.

How often will your prospects need your solution? How easily can they solve the problem? When they want to solve the problem, is it easier to use your solution or do it themselves?

Position your product or service to serve a need that your prospects need over and over again, and you can easily keep a flood of new orders.

Dimension 3: Scope of Desire

The third thing that every profitable mass desire should have is a wide scope, or the number of people who share this desire. For example, the weight loss market has a huge scope, while the number of people who want to play with pet rocks is miniscule in comparison.

When you are advertising, make sure you're advertising to a desire with a vast scope because you want to attract the broadest amount of people in your market so you can get as many leads and sales as possible.

Profiting from Human Nature 101: Common Appeals

If you want to stop guessing about what appeals you should target for your market, pick one of these human desires that have been around since the beginning of time.

Earn Money

Earning money is one of the strongest appeals of all. No matter where you go in the world, you are going to find people who want to earn more to provide a better living for themselves, their families, and to buy whatever their souls desire. Business opportunity offers and stocks are sold using this appeal.

Save Money

When you earn your money, you naturally want to keep more of it. Savings accounts and coupons are sold using this appeal.

Retirement Security

No one wants to worry about day-to-day stresses when he or she is older. You just want to live good, relax, and know that your future is secure. Vacation homes, 401k investments, and the idea of Social Security is sold using this appeal.

Better Health Now

This is why weight loss and health products do so well. People want to have better overall health, and they want to look and feel better, faster.

Professional Advancement

Most people want to move forward in their careers and receive higher pay with more responsibilities. Networking events and like-minded organizations are sold using this appeal.

Prestige

Everyone wants prestige. Most people will not say it, but regardless of the social circle you're in, we all want to look good in front of our peers and have a high social standing. Expensive homes, clothes, shoes, and anything else marketed as "luxury" are sold with this appeal.

Enjoyment

All people want to enjoy life and live good on their terms. Vacations, family outings, and concerts are sold using this appeal.

Easier Life/Chores

People want to have an easier life with less chores and boring responsibilities. Kitchen appliances, cleaning products, and lawn care items are sold using this appeal.

Gain More Leisure

Having more time to relax and unwind is a great buying motivator. Maid services, chefs, and anything that allows you to alleviate work can be sold using this appeal.

Comfort and Convenience

People want to be comfortable and have their needs and wants met conveniently and at their disposal. Drive thru fast food and delivery services are sold using this appeal.

Reduce Body Fat

This one is in the health category, but it's more specific to some people's immediate needs. Diet pills, personal training, gym memberships, and custom meal plans are sold using this appeal.

Freedom From Worry

Worrying sucks. Insurance companies rake in billions yearly by selling the ideas of security and protection- in case something happens.

Desire to be Popular and Attract Attention

We have all done something for the attention of others—this is partly why women wear makeup and jewelry, and why men buy expensive cars.

Desire to be in the "In" Group

Whatever we enjoy or associate with, we all have a desire to be in the "In" group. This could be a fraternity, sorority, sports team, or simply a group of people who go camping together.

Desire to Outshine Your Neighbors

We all have an intrinsic desire to do better than others, but this appeal is best implied rather than spoken. No matter how much people want to out-do others, it's rare that they'll just tell you, "I want to do better than him." This appeal can sell big boats, homes, or anything that can be viewed as a symbol that shows you're doing better than your peers.

Desire for a Bargain

Many folks are always looking for a good deal and good prices. Some businesses rely on price to help customers make their buying decisions, but this works ONLY when you're targeting a prospect who doesn't have disposable income. If you've been doing your homework and following these chapters, you should be targeting affluent clients where price is never a factor.

Walmart is an industry leader that sells on price, and you do not want to compete with them for the "lowest price." It is a terrible idea to compete with any business as a low-price leader because there is always someone willing to undercut you and sacrifice profits.

One final note on appeals: If your appeal becomes overused and outdated, your ads have to change.

Take the dieting industry. If you see an ad that says, "Lose 10 pounds in 10 days," even if you had that desire, it is unlikely that you will respond because that appeal has been used and recycled for many years, and this has killed its selling power.

Once you notice the response to your ads dropping, you need to run new ad tests to see which new appeals will increase your market response.

The USP: Supercharge Your Marketing Message

Having a killer Unique Selling Proposition (USP) will energize your marketing message so you can stand out and outsell many other competing marketing messages.

When you apply the information below, you will be ready to dominate any market you choose.

Ultimate Advantage

The "U" in USP stands for your ultimate advantage. A great question to ask yourself when finding your ultimate advantage is, "What specific benefit do people get from doing business with me that they cannot get from one of my competitors?"

I want to tell you the story about how Levi's denim was born. In 1873 Jacob Davis was listening to customers who were frustrated about the pockets of their work pants repeatedly tearing out.

Davis decided to strengthen the pockets with copper rivets, and these pants became Levi's.

Davis met Mr. Levi and convinced him to do a patent deal partnership, and for the next 35 years Levi's dominated the men's clothing industry because no one else was permitted to place rivets on their jeans.

These men figured out exactly what their target consumers wanted and they gave it to them. When you determine your one major advantage, make sure you emphasize it in everything you do.

Sensational Offer

The "S" in USP stands for sensational offer. When you're thinking about crafting your offers, make a deal that's so good that people will think they're crazy not to take it.

If you remember the Columbia House twelve CDs for a penny offer that used to come in the mail, then you remember one of the most incredible offers of our time.

I remember being a young lad thinking, "How can you sell twelve CDs for a penny? This offer is so irresistible that I have to have it!" I remember running up to my mom and telling her, "Mom, we've got to buy this!"

She was a more savvy shopper than I was at the time so she refused, but that offer always made an impression on my mind.

After I began studying the art of marketing, I found out that Columbia House made their money by automatically enrolling their consumers in a "CD of the Month" club after you took the initial 12 CDs for a penny offer.

The penny offer was used to generate an army of buyers, and they made all of their money on the back-end with $20 monthly membership sales.

You can also create a sensational offer by adding special bonuses to go along with your main product. If you really want to reward and delight people for taking action and buying your product, build enough into your price to send them a surprise bonus just for ordering.

A lot of businesses don't do this, but these small efforts show that you have great customer service and speed of delivery. These are the type of small things that can really take you over the top and allow you to have a more sensational offer than your competitors.

Powerful Promise

The "P" in USP stands for powerful promise. You want to offer a clear, unmistakable, no-questions-asked guarantee *plus a powerful promise.*

One of my mentors, a man by the name of Robert Allen, has a guarantee for his book, *Multiple Streams Of Income*, and it goes like this: "If you haven't earned an extra $10,000 as result of reading *Multiple Streams of Income* in the next 12 months, call the number in the book and I'll personally refund your money and you can keep the book as my gift." This is a huge promise for many reasons, but the most important reason is how it gets people off of the fence to take action and make a purchase.

Another great USP I love comes from the original Domino's Pizza ads. Their USP was "Fresh, hot pizza in 30 minutes or less, or you get your money back. Guaranteed!"

Depending on who your market is, that USP is going to be irresistible. Domino's started out in college towns with a lot of young adults. Domino's doesn't talk about how good the pizza tastes, nor do they boast about how fresh the ingredients are.

They don't make claims like, "We have the best ingredients over Pizza Hut or Papa John's." Domino's merely said they could get a fresh, hot pizza to you in record time. The offer was simple, direct, and it sold a lot of pizzas.

After struggling for many years, this guarantee

single-handedly allowed Domino's to catapult themselves to the top of the pizza industry.

CAUTION: Advertise Only When You Have Something Worth Saying

Remember this lesson: Only advertise when you have something worthwhile to say. A lot of businesses advertise just to tell people their doors are open. They say things like, "Hey everyone! We're in business now!"

This is unfortunate because no one cares.

People have their own things going on, and just because you're in business doesn't mean people care or are affected at all.

I'll take it deeper than that– when you advertise to say, "Hey I'm in business," you're essentially saying, "Come give me your money even though I haven't given you a real reason to do so!"

Advertise when you have a compelling offer.

Advertise when you have something to give that will make people take notice and pay attention.

Get Prospects to Take Action on Your Offers

The last, and arguably the most important part of your headline is the Call to Action. A call to action is simply a direct request to get a prospect to take any kind of action.

You may want someone to send you an email, give you a call, come in for an appointment, or you may want someone to buy immediately. Whatever your desired action, it is your responsibility to tell prospects what you want them to do. The worst mistake you can make is assuming people will take the action you want them to take, without you telling them to take it.

If you look around at the marketplace, you'll see a lot of businesses use brand or image style ads without a call to action. Businesses will have their logos plastered everywhere HOPING that customers will think of their business when they have a specific need.

Hope is a terrible strategy, and it's one of the main reasons a lot of businesses fail.

Brand building has its place, but if you want to track your ad dollars and make sure you are getting a return on every dollar invested, you need to have trackable ads with specific calls to action.

How to Track Ad Profitability

You just learned the importance of having a direct response component to your ad so you can create a trackable ROI for your business. You may be wondering, "Suresh, all of the big companies are doing branding styled ads, why shouldn't I?"

Branding styled ads aren't the best option for small and medium-sized businesses that don't have millions of dollars to throw at building an image and waiting on sales. If you're a small business owner, you need sales *now*. The lifeblood of your business depends on it.

You don't want to just put out a logo and say, "Hey, we're in business, the doors are open," and hope people come when they think about whatever it is that you're selling. You need to make an offer that has a compelling USP that will get cash and repeat business in the doors now.

Every ad that you create will be accountable for bringing in new business. Use these metrics below to ensure that you are making a ROI on your ad spend.

Dollar Per Lead (DPL)

This is simply the calculation that tells you how much it costs to get every new lead in your business.

Here is the formula to calculate DPL:

Ad Cost / Number of new leads from Ad Cost = DPL

For example, let's say your ad cost is $1000, and you get 250 new leads from that ad.

1000 / 250 = $4 DPL

In this example, every new lead you capture costs $4 to acquire.

Dollar Per Customer (DPC)

This calculates how much it costs you to get someone to buy your product or service and become a customer.

Here is the formula to calculate DPC:

Ad Cost / Number of new customers (sales) from Ad Cost = DPC

For example, let's say your ad cost is $1000, and you get 10 new customers from that ad.

1000 / 10 = $100 DPC

In this example, every new customer you capture costs $100 to acquire.

Average Customer Value (ACV)

This is about measuring the *immediate* impact that a specific marketing funnel is having on your business. Unless you're sitting on a mountain of money, you simply can't afford to wait a lifetime to recoup your customer acquisition costs.

Here is the formula to calculate ACV:

Welcome Offer Price + (Main Offer Price * Core Offer Conversion Rate) + (Upsell Price * Upsell Conversion Rate) = Average Customer Value (ACV)

Let's assume you have a $7 Welcome Offer, a $100 Main Offer, and a $400 Upsell. Let's also assume that your Main Offer is converting at 30%, and your Upsell is converting at 10%. Using the equation above, your ACV would be as follows:

$7 + ($100(.3)) + ($400(.1)) = $77 Average Customer Value.

In this example, every time you sell a $7 Welcome Offer, you make $77 in revenue. In other words, you can spend $77 to sell a $7 offer WITHOUT having to go in the red!

Average Visitor Value (AVV)

Average Visitor Value tells how much you can pay for a click. This is essentially your cost to get someone to the beginning of your marketing funnel.

Here is the formula to calculate AVV: Average Customer Value (ACV) * Welcome

Offer Conversion Rate = Average Visitor Value (AVV)

Let's assume that your $7 Welcome Offer is converting at 5%. Using the $77 ACV in the previous example and our equation above, your AVV would be as follows:

$$77 * .05 = \$3.85 \text{ Average Visitor Value (AVV)}$$

This means that you could spend as much as $3.85 per click without going negative!

Once you find out the numbers to these formulas, you'll have enormous value over your competition. When you know how much it costs you to get a new lead, you know how much you can spend to get people to your offer or do your lead generation.

Knowing how much it costs you to acquire your customer reveals how much you can spend on advertising to make a profit.

These numbers are necessary to understand, but a lot of businesses just spend money and hope that they get some kind of return on their investment.

I can't emphasize how important it is that you understand how much you can spend to acquire new customers. Once you learn these figures, you will be able to outspend your competitors; if you can spend more to acquire customers than your competitors can, then it's certain that you will win in business.

* * *

As I was dashing through the airport to fly out and see another client, my phone rang and buzzed loudly.

RING RING RING! It was Claire.

"Hey Suresh!" Claire said with girlish excitement. "What are you doing? I have some great news!"

"Hey Claire! I'm in the airport getting ready to board a plane to New York– please share, I can always use some good news. What's going on?"

"My team and I implemented what you shared during our initial coaching session. Not only are we getting a 0.14% click-through-rate [CTR] on our Facebook ads, we are averaging 461 leads per day, and our landing page is converting at 57.2%!" Claire took a breath and continued. "Our offers weren't converting at all before, and now 3.3% of our prospects are taking our main offer."

"That is great news!" I replied with a smile. I was proud of Claire and her team. They listened and they took fast action.

"After I teach your team about writing sales letters that produce bigger, more profitable results than any army of salesmen, your sales will once again skyrocket."

I hung up with Claire and boarded my plane.

As the plane reached cruising altitude, I stared out of the window and admired the peaceful sky and the pristine clouds. My mind wandered, and I couldn't help but think about how small changes to mobile and internet sales messages can produce massive results.

* * *

In the next chapter, I'll reveal the secret that me and the top digital marketers in the world use to get the best salespeople to work for us nonstop, 24 hours a day.

Massive Action List

1. Write 100 Ads and Headlines For Your Product or Service.

I want you to write 100 ads and headlines to sell your product or service. These don't have to be perfect, it's simply a great exercise to force you to understand the true benefits of your business.

If you can, write 100 different benefits you give the consumer and write an ad around each of those. After you're done, ask your consumers, "Which one of these ads are the most appealling?"

2. Calculate your Dollar per Lead, Dollar per Customer, Average Customer Value, and your Average Visitor Value.

Take some time to figure out your hard numbers so you can visually see the heartbeat of your business. See which advertising vehicles are profitable and which ones are losing money. Learn how much your leads and customers are worth.

Do not delay this process– the profitability of your ad campaign depends on it.

If you want the "35 Proven Formulas for Writing Headlines" cheat sheet, go to www.sureshmay.com/CLCgifts or text your name and email address to 276-565-RICH(7424) and get it for free!

FOUR

How to Sell with Only Ink, Paper, or Pixels

No enterprise can exist for itself alone. It ministers to some great need, it performs some great service, not for itself, but for others…or failing therein, it ceases to be profitable and ceases to exist.
– CALVIN COOLIDGE

ATLANTA, GA

I'VE GIVEN YOU some stories of my clients' business issues and how I've helped them. Now I'd like to share my personal story of struggle and how using sales letters changed my life.

Ink and paper saved me from depression and being dead broke.

I tried business after business, and I interviewed for job after job, but nothing seemed to work on a consistent basis. The stress was mounting, and I almost felt like giving up.

When I finally realized that figuring it out on my own wasn't working, I decided to get a mentor.

But I couldn't get just any mentor, I had to find someone who was in the very upper echelons of the digital marketing field.

I had to get a five-time best-selling author who did 11 multi-million dollar product launches in a row.

I had to get Mike Koenigs.

As I was desperate to get one of the top digital marketers to mentor me, I attached 19 saliva-moistened stamps to 19 handwritten envelopes, and I headed to my local post office full of hope and burning desire.

Why did I send 19 letters? I could only come up with 19 stamps.

In fact, at the time, I didn't have the money to buy the stamps, letters, ink, or the paper my words were printed on. One of these letters had to work.

Mike responded to my direct response letter in three business days.

I wanted mentorship so badly that I would've done anything he asked for free, but he was so impressed with my sales letter that he hired me as a paid consultant.

That $0.49, two-page sales letter yielded a contract with a $50,000,000 client, a contribution to an Amazon instant #1 best-selling book, work on a product launch that earned $1,800,000 in seven days, and the mentorship of a lifetime.

In the chapter that follows, I will reveal how you can use sales letters to get fast, radical results in your business.

Get an Army of Salesmen to Work 24 Hours a Day for Free

I know many of you may be terrified of selling. You may think that you don't know how to do it. You may get so nervous that your palms become sweaty and you get cold feet when it's time to make a sale; but don't worry, you don't have to be afraid.

If you are apprehensive about selling, be confident in the fact that we all sell ourselves every single day. You try to sell your ideas and your thoughts to your friends. When you put on that fresh, single-button, three-piece suit or that beautifully tailored blouse, you're selling yourself to the people around you.

Think about this for a moment: How would you feel if you could create something one time that sold for years and years in the future? What if you had thousands of salesmen selling for you day and night? What if these salesmen never complained, took a sick day, or called off?

What if you could take your pen, a piece of paper, or pixels on your computer screen and create content that sold for you over and over again *forever*? This would eliminate the excruciating task of cold calling and cold prospecting from your business forever.

If you haven't figured it out by now, I'm talking about writing sales letters. To put it simply, writing effective sales letters is the most crucial skill that separates people who are successful selling on the internet and mobile platforms from those who struggle.

If you want to have long lasting success selling on the internet and mobile devices, you have to learn how to write killer cash copy. Having the ability to write cash copy gives you the ultimate leverage because you can do the work once, and if you combine it with the targeting and advertising skills you've learned in previous chapters, your sales letter can literally sell for you until the end of time.

All you have to do is create a great ad that sends traffic to your offer–this can come from online ad platforms, direct mail campaigns, email traffic, etc.–no matter the traffic source, your letter can convert leads into sales as effectively as 100 salaried salesman.

Mastering the Markets = Mastering the Money

The old cliche "actions speak louder than words" is dead-on when it comes to understanding what markets are willing to buy. If you want to hit the bullseye and sell things that you know people are buying, you need to make a habit of studying what people *are* buying versus what they *say* they will buy.

People have buying trends, and you can easily see what people are actually pulling out their credit cards and spending money on. If you go to a focus group and ask a group of people for feedback on your product or service, most people will be nice and say, "Oh, yeah, I think that's a great idea," even if they think it's terrible.

If you ask those same people to pull out their credit cards and make a buying decision, most of them won't do it. Before you spend the time, money, and energy to create a product, put your sales letter to the test and see if people will take action and vote with their wallets.

The "Guaranteed Results" Marketing Triangle

One of the smartest marketing minds in the world, Dan Kennedy, created the famous Results Triangle. The Results Triangle is when you have the right media, the right message, and the right market in place, creating a marketing sweet spot to effectively sell your product and service.

When you have all three of these elements aligned, you can really begin to dominate markets with your sales letter.

Right Media

Find out where your ideal clients spend most of their time. When you figure out where your market congregates, you'll want to spend most of your advertising budget in that media.

This could mean that you're buying Facebook, Google, or Twitter ads; or it could mean that you should advertise in a magazine or another more traditional media. If you find that most of your prospects hang out at a certain blog or niche website, do not get caught up in spending a lot of your ad budget on a social media site because it's "hot and new."

When business owners begin to advertise, most of them only use one to three different types of media to find their customers. This strategy can work as you're starting out, but you want to begin using as many forms of media as you possibly can, as soon as you can. I have my clients use at least 10 to 20 media outlets for their messages. Using more media outlets for your sales letters will allow you to get more leads and sales in record time.

Right Message

The second thing you must have is the right message for your target market. One of the most important factors in having the right message is specificity. When your messages are specific to your target market, they have a much greater impact than if you use general messaging in an attempt to capture a broad market.

After you begin targeting your desired market, you'll find that you're going to need different messages to send to the different subgroups of that market. For instance, if you're focused on a weight loss market, you should quickly notice that this market has two major sub groups with vastly different desires: men and women.

If you're focused on the women, you may need to center your messaging around fat loss around love handles, thighs, and arms.

But if you're speaking to a man, your message should not be the same as talking to a woman. You may want to talk about getting lean, ripped abs, broad, strong shoulders, and bulging biceps.

You could possibly have the same product for every subgroup that you're targeting, just make sure that your messaging fits their respective desires.

Right Market

I discussed this extensively in Chapter 1, and I'll stress the importance again here: You MUST pick the right market. Who do you want to respond to your ads? Who is your ideal customer? Who are your best customers?

You need to have all of these things identified in your business to make sure that you have the right market.

A lot of business owners go into business and attempt to sell to people who can't buy or who can't make buying decisions. Sometimes these same business owners target customers who have to make a tough buying decision because they don't have much disposable income.

These types of consumers cannot be your ideal customer. You need someone who has a lot of disposable income and who can make huge buying decisions.

Do You Know What's on Your Customers' Minds?

Great sales letters always start with the customer in mind. When writing your sales letter, open up by talking about the most dominant desire in your prospect's mind.

If you're selling diet pills, people aren't walking around saying, "I need ABC diet pills to help me lose weight." People are saying "I want to lose weight around my belly, I want to get leaner, I want to get ripped, I want to get a stronger chest."

Remember, no one cares about you or your product, they only care about the solutions your product brings.

Let's say you're an owner of a martial arts studio and you want parents to sign their kids up for your classes. If you advertise your martial arts studio as is, you may get some people to take advantage of your offer, but the people who do will be highly interested in martial arts.

In addition to self defense, martial arts studios teach discipline, strength training, and self control. These are some of the benefits that you may want to advertise because you will pique the interests of parents who want to see these attributes in their kids.

The parent is making the buying decision, so you might run an ad with a headline that reads, "How to Get Your Children to be More Disciplined So They Perform Better in School."

That's something that a lot of parents will be interested in because you know a child's performance in school is at the top of most parents' minds. If a parent has a child who is having problems at school because he or she lacks discipline, this ad is going to strike a nerve. Your headline is going to pull parents in and make them want to read your advertisement. After you pull them in, that's when you start to talk about the benefits of martial arts and how they will help a student improve.

The key thing to understand is that parents don't initially have to be interested in martial arts. They just have to be interested in that big benefit, which is helping their child improve in school *through* martial arts.

This is one of the biggest things people miss in

advertising: Your target customer doesn't have to be interested in the product that you're selling, they just have to be interested in the *benefits* they'll reap from your product.

The Single Most Reliable Marketing Tool

If done correctly, a sales letter can become your ultimate business asset. After you write one good sales letter, it can replace your entire sales force, and in a lot of instances, a sales letter can replace business development reps who are focused on cold lead generation for you.

When you sit down to write your sales letter, make sure that it is very specific and that it has every detail your target prospect is going to want to hear about.

Your sales letter is going to give you massive leverage, but you have to make sure that you are touching on all the positives and the pain points your target customers have.

Whatever marketing mediums you're currently using, sales letters translate to all of them. It doesn't matter if you want to advertise online, offline, radio, or on TV, a sales letter can be used to boost your business.

Fool-Proof Formulas for Writing Words that Sell

If this is your first time writing a sales letter, worry not. I'm going to give you two very common sales formulas that superstar marketers use when writing their million dollar sales letters.

Attention, Interest, Desire, Action

The first sales letter formula is called Attention, Interest, Desire, and Action, or AIDA for short.

The **attention** part is designed to grab your market's attention with your headlines and opening paragraphs. You want to grab them by the collar with whatever problem they have, or whatever their strongest desires are.

Secondly, make them **interested** in what you're about to sell. Talk about what they need, talk about the benefits of your solution, and talk about how you will solve their problems.

The third part of AIDA is **desire**. You want to ramp up that desire– make the desire burn inside of them so much that they *have to have* what you're selling. You can set their desires on fire by talking about how life will be after they have the solution you're offering.

Lastly, you need to get prospects to take **action**. You have to have some sort of call to action– whether that means buying your product, filling out a form to generate a lead, or calling in for an appointment. You have to tell the prospect what you want them to do *and* how to do it.

Problem, Agitate, Solve

The second major sales formula is called Problem, Agitate, Solve.

This sales formula consists of exposing the biggest **problem** your prospect is having–it lets prospects know you understand their pain.

After establishing that you know what your prospects are going through, **agitate** the problem to make it seem bigger than it actually is. This step is key because you have to make sure people really want to find a solution after reading your copy.

After you've successfully added a little salt to your consumers' wounds, you can then offer a solution that **solves** the problem and cures their pain.

The above formulas are to get you started. Once you begin crafting your letter, here are some additional elements that you need to create compelling sales copy:

Find the Hook

You have to get a hook that will keep your prospects interested in your sales message. What's the interesting story? What is the main benefit that will keep your reader engaged until the end?

What can you tie into your sales message that has a current news element?

State Your Reasons

Anytime you tell people that you're going to do something for their benefit, you need to give a reason why. Telling people why is very persuasive, and it converts more sales. For example, when you see businesses advertising sales because they are going out of business, that's "reason why" in action.

Stay Active

There is a major difference between telling someone, "*When* you get [a benefit]…" versus "*If* you get [a benefit]…" Don't say, "You *could* have [a benefit]." Instead, say, "You *will* have [a benefit]."

Using confident language makes a huge difference, and these psychological subtleties will improve your sales copy.

Another one of the problems many of my clients have is they are very passive in their copy. They say, "*If* you do this…" or "You *could* have this…" and "*Maybe* if this works out for you…" We want to make sure that we are speaking to prospects in a way that firmly suggests they're going to get the benefit they want after consuming our product or service.

Use Conversational Writing

Write as if you're talking to an old friend. Just relax and have a conversation. If you're trying to write like a professor, your message will not resonate and people will not respond favorably. Talk to people the way they actually speak to each other.

Reverse Risks

Risk reversals are key in making sales with people who are on the fence. Be sure to make it as easy as possible for people to take action and buy your products and services. You can reverse the risk by giving 100% money back guarantees, double your money back guarantees, or you can add bonuses simply for purchasing. When thinking of ways to reverse your client's risks, you are only limited by your imagination.

Make Guarantees

Another thing you want to have in your sales copy are mind-blowing guarantees. As I mentioned in an earlier chapter, one of my favorite guarantees is from Domino's Pizza– when they first started out, their guarantee was, "Fresh, hot pizza in 30 minutes or less. Guaranteed!"

If Domino's didn't get your pizza to you in 30 minutes or less, you were guaranteed to get your money back *and* a free pizza. It's an incredible guarantee, and when they began using that unique selling proposition, it helped their business skyrocket.

Include Proof Elements

Testimonials and proof that you can deliver are crucial to your success on the internet and mobile devices. You want people saying they like your product or your service, but powerful testimonials have to be crafted in a certain way.

A lot of people write terrible testimonials. When you're crafting your testimonials, they have to be benefit-driven. Base your testimonials on the end result your target customer wants from your product or service, and think of any objections people may have that will prevent them from buying. Make your testimonials address desires and concerns, and you'll have proof that will trump your competitors.

If you're selling a diet pill, a prospect may come to your site and think, "I've done workouts and diet pills in the past and they just kind of didn't work for me." Anticipate your prospects' objections, and address them in your testimonials.

Crafting testimonials that sell is important, however, I'm not giving you license to make up fake testimonials! All of your testimonials need to be authentic, and they should also aid in the sales process.

If you can, get a testimonial from a current customer that addresses the exact objections you know your market will bring up.

The testimonial may read: "I got burned in the past from using different diet products, but I used this one and it helped me achieve X results in Y amount of time and it really works."

That's a powerful testimonial. It addresses the objection, it has the result your market wants, and it lets you know how long it might take a customer to achieve the desired result.

Usually you see testimonials say something like, "This product is great, you should try it!" That testimonial is horrible because it doesn't offer a single benefit, nor does it overcome any kind of objection that prospects may have going through your sales funnel.

If your product is new and no one has tried it, give your product away for free to get real, honest testimonials.

Adding customers' names creates another layer of authenticity to your testimonials. You may also want to use a person's occupation, website (if he or she has one), and his or her picture.

If you've been involved in any media, include those credentials as well. If you've been on television or radio, or associated with any of your market's notable celebrities, incorporate proof of this (in the form of photos or links to interviews) into your sales letter.

Give Strong Calls to Action

Again, be sure to have a call to action in your sales letter. The biggest mistake businesses make is not telling the prospect what they want them to do. You can't assume they're going to take action; you have to explicitly ask prospects to take your desired action.

Add Persuasive Bonuses

Add bonuses that make your offer irresistible. If you're selling a diet pill, you can give away free workouts, meal plans, or a fat caliper to measure body fat. Whatever you decide to give away, make sure it's related to your product and that it has a high perceived value.

Long Copy vs Short Copy?

When it comes to writing sales letters, a lot of people ask, "Should I have a long or short-form sales letter?"

The length of your sales letter doesn't really matter. The most important thing is to make sure it's long enough to tell your entire sales story. Would you tell your salespeople to sell your product using only 50 words? Of course you wouldn't do that! You would tell your people to say any and everything they need to say to get the product sold. Think about that when you're writing ads and sales copy.

Don't shorten your message because you think people won't read it. People read what they are interested in. That's why books continue to do well! As long as your product or service fulfills your target market's needs and wants, prospects will be interested. Make your copy as long as it needs to be.

How to Persuade People to Buy

There's a great book by Dr. Robert Cialdini called *Influence*, in which he talks about the six psychological principles that persuade people to take action. Most people are unaware any of these principles are taking place because they are automatic. Add these tools to your sales letters and marketing funnels and watch your sales soar.

1. Law of Reciprocity

The first principle is the Law of Reciprocity. The Law of Reciprocity says we should repay in kind what another person has given us. Most of us take pride in being nice, giving people because being nice and giving has a high value in society.

If a friend of yours does a nice thing for you, naturally you're going to want to do something back for them. This feeling of "paying it forward" is usually automatic, and that's where the Law of

Reciprocity kicks in.

If you're doing a free lead generation offer in your sales process, people naturally want to give things back to you. As a business owner, the best gift people can give you is their business. And here's the great thing about reciprocity: the exchange doesn't have to be even. If you give someone a freebie, they will not give you a freebie back. If you deliver with a great product or service, people will give you money in exchange for solving their problems.

2. Commitment and Consistency

The second principle deals with commitment and consistency. This one works because our desire to appear consistent with what we have already done is a strong psychological trigger. If you take an action and you commit to doing something, you want to appear consistent to your peers.

If you get people in your marketing funnel by having them take a free or low-priced offer, they are more likely to buy your core offer just to appear consistent with what they've already done.

3. Social Proof

Thirdly, consider social proof. This principle basically means that if other people like it, we will usually like it too. When you see a long line in a movie theatre, you automatically assume the movie is good.

If you ask friends, "What do you think about this?" you're looking for acceptance and assurance, or social proof.

4. Liking

We must consider likability when thinking of principles of persuasion. We prefer to say "yes" to requests from someone we know, trust, and like.

5. Authority

The fifth principle is authority. People easily and willingly follow experts, and this is why you must position your business as an expert in its market. If you can be perceived as an expert, you will get higher-paying clients, you will have lower resistance to your sales offers, and people will naturally take your word as truth.

I'm always amazed by people who adopt the words of others without doing any of their own research, but this simply illustrates the power of authority.

6. Scarcity

Scarcity is the final principle of persuasion. Simply put, opportunity is deemed to be more valuable when it has a limited availability. Take dating, for instance. I constantly hear people say, "Since

I started dating this woman/man, it seems as if everyone wants to date me now! Where were all of these potential relationships when I was single?" You're now finding so many people interested in you *because* you're taken. We tend to covet things we can't have, and it makes us take action when we think something is scarce or that it will be taken away from us.

When you make sales offers, you need to have deadlines, low inventory, or whatever truth you need to make people get off their asses and take action. After you implement a deadline in your business, you'll get more people to get off the fence and take action and buy.

Massive Action Items

1. Write a rough draft of a sales letter.

Include every element that was discussed in this chapter in your sales letter. The most important thing is to JUST DO IT. Try! If this is your first time writing a sales letter, odds are that it won't be great. That's totally fine. Just like the first time you rode a bike without training wheels, you likely fell, dusted yourself off, and started riding again. Keep writing, and your sales letters are sure to improve. Have fun with it!

If you do not have the desire to write a sales letter for yourself, you can always hire my team to write a winning sales letter for you.

If you want to create an army of sales reps selling for you, get the 21-step sales letter checklist at www.sureshmay.com/CLCgifts or text your name and email address to 276-565-RICH(7424) and get it for free!

Section 2:
How to Make
Customers Spend
More Money

FIVE

How to Make People Buy Everything You Sell

The NBA is never just a business. It's always business. It's always personal. All good businesses are personal. The best businesses are very personal.
– MARK CUBAN

DALLAS, TX

TO SAY TRACY was frustrated and pissed was an understatement.

She was beginning to resent her decision to become an entrepreneur, and she flirted with the thought of giving it all up and submitting her soul to be sucked by a lifeless, meaningless day job. At least, that's what a day job felt like to her: lifeless, meaningless, and menial.

After trying her hand at a dog grooming business (the ill-fated Dirty Doggy), and an all natural hair dye line (the headache-inducing

Homemade Hair Henna- ever tried to be taken seriously with blue hands?), this was the third business she'd "launched" that produced little to no results, and Tracy had no idea what was wrong.

Well, this was *sort of* her third business launch. Tracy had decided to return to Dirty Doggy. But this time, she hoped to attract affluent dog lovers who could easily spend tens of thousands of dollars on their dogs annually. She hoped to accomplish this by creating an exclusive doggy membership program.

The problem Tracy faced her first two times around was so simple and yet so easy to miss, most entrepreneurs and business owners do it every day: Tracy created a product or service first and attempted to fill the demand second.

This is the ultimate losing strategy, and she learned the hard way.

Tracy's desperation eventually led her to purchase the *Lifetime Customer Blueprint* training program, and what she learned about making products virtually irresistible will blow you away!

If you want to avoid wasting your time and money creating products that do not sell, then this chapter is for you.

The Best Marketing Advice You'll Ever Get

If you are anything like me, you have a lot of money-making ideas. And, perhaps, when you come up with what you believe to be an amazing idea, you automatically think everyone else is going to love it, too.

So you build upon that idea. You invest your time, your energy, your money, your blood, your sweat, and your tears to create your dream product. At the apex of your excitement, you beautifully package the fruit of your labor and put it on the market.

But it bombs. No one buys it.

You get zero leads.

You thought this idea was the proverbial new wheel, so what happened?

You failed because you created a product or service based on what *you* wanted to create. You failed because you created a product or service without asking your market what *it* needed or wanted.

To help prevent this problem in the future, I'm going to give you the best three-step marketing advice to guarantee success:

1. Find the right audience
2. Ask people what they want
3. Give people what they want

In Chapter 1 we covered the importance of targeting an affluent consumer. Your target audience needs to have the ability and willingness to buy, and they need to be affordably reachable.

In addition to these target audience qualifications, pick an audience that is already in a feeding frenzy. Choose a group of people who already want what you will sell them. Your goal isn't to *convince* people to buy your product or service; your goal is to create a product or service that *meets the needs of your market so well that people can't help but to buy it.*

The second step you must take is asking people what they want. One of my favorite lines to tell my consulting clients is, "Ask to get." If you want something in life, it's usually as simple as asking for it.

Before you even think about creating your next product, I want you to reverse the process that most business owners take. Instead of jumping the gun like an anxious track star, ask your market, "What do you want? What do you need?"

These simple questions will give you all of the necessary information to create a product that sells quickly and easily.

After the people in your affluent market tell you what they want, give it to them. This system for creating products is so simple and profound, I'm still amazed at how many businesses do not use it.

Listen: I gave you the secret to product creation,

so stop burning ad dollars with a *hope* strategy. DO NOT create a product *then* go looking for someone to sell it to.

Please do not confuse this marketing advice by thinking that I'm saying you can never create demand. You can create demand, but it's easier to create wealth when you jump into the flow of where people are already spending money.

When you find your market first, the people in it will buy your product or service because you're giving them *exactly* what they want.

This product creation method trumps all others because you're not guessing, hoping, wishing, and praying for success. Selling people on hope may win elections, but it's a terrible business strategy.

Four Major Ask Campaign Questions

Before you run your ask campaign, there are four major questions to answer:

1: Who should I sell to?

2: What do they actually want?

3: What are their pain points?

4: What words do they use to describe their desired product or service?

As you run your ask campaign, your market will reveal itself and let you know which segment of the market you should sell to.

Prospects in your market will tell you exactly what they want, and they're going to tell you all about their pain points.

Lastly, when people send you questions and concerns, you'll notice key words and phrases they use to describe their issues. Pay attention to these because this feedback is a gold mine for your sales copy. This information will allow you to turn their pain points into benefit-driven sentences that sell.

* * *

This time around Tracy knew she would succeed because she listened to the needs of her market. When Dirty Doggy relaunched, Tracy grossed $1,720,000 in sales in one month!

* * *

If you ask your market the correct questions before you create your product, it will give you a license to serve its needs and create an indefinite amount of wealth.

Massive Action Items

1. Create an Ask Campaign.

Launch a simple lead generation ad campaign and ask one simple question, "What's your biggest problem with X?"

Poll your customers and they'll give you answers. Find at least 100 answers and outline the responses. You'll notice many redundant responses, and that's perfectly fine. These repeating opinions will be the most important part of your new data-driven product.

If you would like to see a live ask campaign page that you can model for your business, go to www.sureshmay.com/CLCgifts or text your name and email address to 276-565-RICH(7424) and get it for free!

SIX

How to Sell High-Priced Products & Services

Live daringly, boldly, fearlessly. Taste the relish to be found in competition – in having put forth the best within you.
– HENRY J. KAISER

PITTSBURGH, PA

"DAMN!" BILLY SHOUTED as he slammed his laptop's monitor closed.

"*Only 5%*? That's terrible!" Billy complained loudly to himself.

Since he knows he has an amazing dating e-book with awesome reviews, his anger grew because he isn't making a big profit.

At the publication of *How to Create Lifetime Customers*, Billy has sold 7,154 copies of his e-book, and customers are demanding more.

Billy left his desk and ventured to the couch

to sprawl out. He usually spoke to himself aloud to clear his thoughts, so he continued his rant. "Everyone loves my book, but I can't figure out why they aren't taking my upsell. I know the price is low enough to make people buy it, so why is it not working? This is ridiculous."

After a few lifeless hours on the couch, Billy bounced up as if he was suddenly struck by lightning.

Even though he had been taught better, Billy was afraid to add high-end prices to his products because he feared his customers would no longer buy.

Billy created a DVD to upsell his dating book clients, but less than 5% of his customers took the offer.

Billy was disappointed, and rightfully so: Anything less than a 30% conversion is a dead giveaway that you're leaving a ton of money behind.

"I need to raise my prices and give more results. I know that's it," Billy finally spoke with confidence. "Suresh taught us this in the *Lifetime Customer Blueprint* training program, and I simply haven't implemented what I've learned." After Billy made this confession to himself, he brightened up for the first time all day.

He finally decided to do what he already knew he needed to do, and he made a mental commitment.

"I'm going to take the next 7 days to restructure my main offer, and I'm going to crush it."

The following chapter reveals how he did just that.

* * *

Profit BIG by Giving Customers Results In Advance

If you've studied any of the top internet marketers over the last ten years, you have probably noticed that they sell products priced as high as $10,000 *on the internet*.

If you have ever looked on in amazement and wondered, "How in the hell do they do that?", you are in for a treat.

Selling high ticket products online can be VERY difficult if you attempt to do it in a traditional "sell first, value second" way. To be successful in the digital era, you have to give value first, and get sales second.

A wonderful sales concept known as Results in Advance makes it easy to sell anything online, no matter the price.

Results in Advance works like this: Before you ask for a sale, take your prospects through a series of big, high-impact results.

Assume we are operating in the dating

market. Let's say we are selling a $1,997 dating product that teaches men how to meet beautiful women, take them out on dates, and build lasting relationships.

The first thing you want to identify on this journey are the Four Major Milestones a guy must graduate through in order to achieve his goal of taking a woman on a date.

While in a social setting, if a man sees a woman he'd like to get to know and possibly take on a date, the first thing he needs to do is say, "Hello." Our example takes place in a social setting because *most* women are not interested in being stopped in the streets. A shy guy would be more likely to meet women at a social gathering.

This may seem like an elementary step, but many guys are scared shitless when faced with the prospect of approaching women and saying anything.

Some guys are extremely shy, and it doesn't get easier when you consider the fact that a number of women are apprehensive about conversing with random men.

Plus, some women are so breathtakingly beautiful that they give bashful guys cement shoes and the blues.

It can be rough out there for shy guys!
Onward.

On the first value step, we can teach the gentleman a foolproof way of saying "hello" without getting rejected.

After he gives his proper, respectful introduction, step two would be to have an intelligent, interesting conversation with the woman.

Think about it: After you say hello to her, what are you going to say next? How are you going to keep her engaged and interested in what you are saying? In our sequence, we can offer the solution to this issue.

At this point we have approached a beautiful woman, started talking to her (and she is talking back!), and now we want to close the deal in step three: Ask her for her phone number.

We can teach our guy a smooth way to try to get a woman's number if she seems open to his advances, or we can teach him how to gracefully bow out if her body language and conversation are screaming, "Leave me alone!"

In the fourth step, after he gets the number, you can teach him how to call her up and get her to go on a great date.

See how easy that is?

When you give your prospects the solutions to the four major milestones before you ask them to buy your product, your prospects will treat you like royalty.

Once you give them this pure value, you will build a mountain of trust, you will gain a lot of credibility, and you will be viewed as the authority.

The closer you bring people to their desired goal, the greater their desire for more becomes. You want to make people say, "Okay, what do I do now?" When your prospects begin asking for more, they will be primed to buy whatever you sell them.

As you are covering these four major milestones, be sure to make your solutions content-driven. The content you produce can be videos, audios, webinars, teleseminars, or even PDFs. If you have to pick one, go with TV. TV or video is the best option because it creates a celebrity-style credibility.

After you finish delivering your Results in Advance, it's time to make your offer. All you need to do to ask for the sale is tell people what you have, tell them *how* your product or service is going add value to their lives, then ask them to buy. It's just that simple.

The Higher You Ascend, the More They Spend

One of the most bizarre things I have learned about selling online is this: People will pay more money for the same information if you package it a different way.

For example, if you start on the lower end of the Lead Lifeline with an e-book for $10, you can repackage that information into a webinar, charge more money for it, and people will still buy it.

Personally, I've bought books, audio books, and even DVDs that have the same information in them. I bought all of them so that I could consume them depending on what I was doing, and your prospects are no different.

Whether you are selling an e-book or a done-for-you service, people have various levels of needs and receive information differently, and they will gladly pay more for an enriching experience.

Most of your leads will begin at the bottom of the Lead Lifeline, so let's begin there.

The Nine Profitable Steps in the Lead Lifeline

Once you get a new lead in your sales and marketing funnel, you have to mature people through the lifeline. Maturing customers through the lifeline allows you to build a lasting relationship, offer continuous value, and steadily increase your profits in nine simple steps.

Step 1: Pre-frame

The first step is the pre-frame, and this is, essentially, deciding how people will feel when they come in contact with *you*.

What are people learning about you?

How are they perceiving you before they are

introduced to your products and services? Create your desired image so your prospects will view you exactly how you want them to.

Step 2: Pleasure or Pain

In order to make the most out of the pre-frame step, you need to know if your customers are moving toward pleasure or if they're moving away from pain.

A lot of people don't understand the difference between these two sentiments, but "pleasure or pain" simply means that you must understand your prospects' buying motives. Is your customer trying to achieve some sort of happiness, or is your customer trying to alleviate a painful situation?

For example, let's say you have two guys you want to sell your diet pills to. One guy may be trying to get leaner and more ripped so he can look good on a beach. This is a pleasure motive.

On the other hand, the other guy may be morbidly overweight, depressed, and has experienced bullying because of his weight. This prospect will buy your product to move away from pain.

Apply "pleasure or pain" to your funnel sequence. Understand the various sales angles you need to implement with your product depending on what kind of person is coming through your funnel.

Step 3: Identifying Buyers

After you make your lead generating offer, you should make a second low-priced offer to find out who is willing to spend money. The optimal price for a low-cost offer is $1-$10. The whole purpose is to see who will pull out their credit cards and make a buying decision. Buyers are more valuable, so we want to find out who they are as early as possible.

Step 4: Continuity

In marketing and sales, it's widely said that if you don't have continuity in your business, you don't really *have* a business. Having a continuity business adds predictable revenue to your bottom line, and it prevents you from frustratingly trying to find new customers every month.

Step 5: Ascension Model

The ascension model is when you add "levels" or "packages" to your offer. I'm sure you have seen companies offer a silver, gold, or even a platinum package. These package upsells offer huge profit potential. Effectively implemented upsells can see 30% or more customers take the higher level "package" offer.

Step 6: Identify Hyper Active Buyers

The sixth step to creating a more profitable lead

line is identifying your hyperactive buyers. Simply offer both upsells and downsells in your funnel and take notice of who makes multiple buying decisions.

When you identify the people who are buying your introductory offer, your main offer, and your upsells and downsells, you will have found a group of prospects that are going to be more valuable than all the rest.

Step 7: Change the Environment (Break the Pattern)

If you're selling to people online, you may want to take your customers offline. This creates a pattern interrupt in the way customers are used to buying from you, and it can increase sales when you take people out of their comfortable buying zones.

Step 8: Age the Lead

After your customers have made a purchase, you'll surely want to sell them the next logical upsell, but it is very important that you do this at the correct time.

For example, if you're selling a solution to a problem and someone buys, and you *then* try to sell another "part" of the solution too quickly, that customer may react unfavorably and you may lose a lot of sales.

People will think, "I *just* bought this

initial product from you– is this incomplete or something?" To avoid creating irate customers, pace your big ticket upsells, and sell products that can be combined versus selling similar or identical products.

Step 9: Sell Up the Value Ladder

Earlier I told you that people will pay more money for the same content packaged a different way. Check out this list below so you can get some ideas of what you can upsell in your business.

1. Free reports and free videos
2. Paid e-books and books
3. Audio and video programs
4. Home study courses
5. Live seminars
6. One-on-one coaching
7. Done-for-you services
8. Software
9. Product extensions

No matter what you are selling, if you send people through an ascension model and follow the lead lifeline, you will undoubtedly get truly transformational results in your business.

* * *

Billy rushed back to his desk to recreate his high ticket product. He started out selling his product for only $100, but after his lesson in giving customers Results in Advance, he raised the price to $997.

After his launch a week later, this price increase and change in product positioning bumped his sales up by 361%, and his upsell was now converting at a whopping 42%.

As he called his friend Arthur to tell him the good news, Billy was thrilled. He knew he could do it, and the exponential bump in his profits per customer kept a smile on his face for a very long time.

* * *

Profiting when people say yes is fun—but do you want to know what's really cool? Getting people to buy more after they say no.

The key to achieve this is in the following chapter, and trust me, if recovering "lost" sales are important to you, you don't want to miss it.

Massive Action Items

1. Brainstorm products you want to sell to ascend people up your value ladder.

Whatever business you're in, think about the suite

of products you will sell to ascend people through your funnel. Make a quick outline of your free reports and videos. Think about an e-book or book you can write to enhance your product or service.

Map these things out and start implementing them in your business right away. The faster you implement, the faster you will profit and create massive wealth.

To see a Results in Advance campaign in action, go to www.sureshmay.com/LCB or text your name and email address to 276-565-RICH(7424) and see a master marketing funnel for free!

SEVEN

How to Maximize Profits in Your Business

Whatever the mind of man can conceive and believe, it can achieve. Thoughts are things! And powerful things at that, when mixed with definiteness of purpose, and burning desire, can be translated into riches.
– NAPOLEON HILL

LAS VEGAS, NV

H E NEVER UNDERSTOOD why he continued to lose sales while his competitors were doubling their business.

The only thing David knew for sure was that he needed to plug his business's leaks and do it *fast*.

David was bummed out, so as he took a seat at his mastermind meeting, he discreetly asked Jim for advice.

"Jim, I'm having a hard time keeping customers in my marketing funnels. My profit per customer value is plummeting, and I do not know what I should offer to get my customers to make more purchases."

"Well," Jim said in a whisper, "I went to the *Lifetime Customer Blueprint* seminar last week and I learned how to partner with other businesses to do successful cross-sells and promotions."

David's entire energy changed as his eyes lit up. "I know that I can do a better job with my upsells, but I never considered partnering with other companies and cross-selling products! That may be exactly what I need to spice up my offerings without having to create something new."

As the mastermind meeting came to a close, David left with a little more pep in his step. He had a simple solution to a complex problem, and he was ready to get to work.

As David found out, you don't have to always be in creation mode to make more sales in your business- sometimes all it takes is a little leverage from other people's offers.

Whether you need a bump offer, upsell, downsell, or cross-sell, in this chapter you'll discover how to profitably enact all of these and more.

The Easiest Way to Make More Money in Your Business

One of the most classic money-making lines in the history of business is, "Do you want fries with that?"

If you find yourself getting fat at McDonald's, take notice of the classic "Do you want an extra amount of X?" bump offer. The cashier casually asks you to bump up your order, and a lot of people comply.

On the surface, that extra $0.50 may look like a small transaction, but when that figure is multiplied by the millions of people who take the offer everyday, profits for the fast food restaurant giant increase exponentially.

Not only do upsells give you a potent profit multiplier, many businesses need upsells to survive, break even, and even profit.

McDonald's spends millions (if not billions) in advertising to get customers into their restaurants. When you go to one of the restaurants to order a combo or a few sandwiches from the Dollar Menu, odds are McDonald's is operating at a loss or barely breaking even on that purchase.

There are great costs to getting new customers in its restaurant, so it's a strong possibility that McDonald's needs upsells to make a profit.

In the early years when I first attacked the business learning curve, the thing that kept Uber

Human Institute afloat was installing a monthly, no-hassle auto-billing feature to ship my clients a new bottle of UBERQUICK.

I was a little apprehensive about adding the feature, but to my pleasant surprise, about 47% of my clients took the offer. Many customers stayed in the auto-billing program for twelve to fifteen months, and they raved about getting new product every month without having to manually reorder.

Upsells

When crafting upsells, make sure they are a natural extension to your front-end offer. When you order a burger at McDonald's, it makes sense for them to offer fries with your order.

If McDonald's began offering an oil change with your burger, customers would find that ridiculous, and almost no one would take the oil change offer.

I recently bought a $7 checklist that promised to teach me how to "...get [my] first 1000 customers and maximize the profits from [my] blog".

As soon as I purchased this product, I was immediately taken to a page that read, "Here's how to move beyond your first 1,000 customers."

The upsell was valued at $150, and it was positioned as a great complementary product to the initial $7 front-end offer.

When savvy marketers offer products this way,

there is a lot of persuasive psychology at play.

After a prospect takes the "front-end welcome offer" for less than $10, that person has qualified him or herself as a buyer. Once prospects are qualified, it becomes easier to sell them a big ticket item.

I study a ton of marketing offers, and as I went through this funnel, I immediately noticed how my psychology changed after I bought the $7 product. Although I didn't buy the upsell (I was only studying the funnel), the $7 purchase warmed me up to being sold more products.

Another important point about upsells is that they do not have to be separate from your core offer. In the previous example, the $7 product was a small piece of the $150 offer. The $7 offer promised to help you get your first 1000 customers, and the big ticket product expounded on that to help you get beyond 1000 customers.

Upsells can be created very, very quickly. These can be audios, videos, PDFs, or can be a different version of what you are selling on the front-end. Do not overthink it– simply start creating or partnering with other businesses who have supplementary products in place.

Downsells

The opposite of the upsell is the downsell. The downsell usually consists of a price break or trial offer, but it can also be a totally new offer.

There are many ways to position the downsell, but the goal is to try to convert the people who didn't take the upsell on a low-risk offer. If you can get people to take your downsell, you will keep them in your marketing funnel and increase your profit per customer.

Bump Offers

A bump offer is similar to an upsell, but these are usually shown right on the checkout page immediately before an order is processed. The bump offer is the closest thing to a fast food cashier asking you to Super Size your order.

Affiliate Offers

A great way to create an upsell without having to create another product is using affiliate offers. Affiliate marketing is selling other people's products and making a commission.

Whichever offers you decide to sell, always remember the difference between front-end and back-end offers.

The front-end offer is what you sell prospects in the beginning of your sales funnel. This is usually a low-ticket offer that begins the buying process. If front-end offers give customers the opportunity to take the small step towards buying from you, then the back-end offer allows them to take a gaping leap, and it allows *you* to make huge profits!

When advertising your offers, it's important to note that you can lose money on the front-end and still have a profitable campaign as long as your back-end marketing funnel is set up properly.

A lot of business owners stop advertising too soon because they aren't making money on their front-end offers. The profitability of your ad campaigns depend on your customer acquisition cost, cost per lead, and your cost per sale. As explained before, stopping an ad campaign too early is short-sided because most of the money made in businesses come from back-end offers and upsells.

Add one or more of these features to your business and be sure to test it before you give up prematurely on what could be a wildly profitable campaign.

* * *

After a few months of testing and building relationships with JV partners, the profits in David's Contemporary Bespoke Man custom clothing business were soaring. He teamed up with a local shoe merchant to cross-sell custom leather shoes when his current customers came to get fitted for new clothes.

37% of his clients bought custom shoes, and

David didn't have to spend a dime to make that extra $622,000 he made that year.

* * *

Take a page from David's playbook. When you're implementing the action items at the end of this chapter, think of creative ways to add to your bottom line.

Massive Action Items

1. Brainstorm welcome offers, upsells, downsells, etc.

Think about complementary products that can be put together to add more value and make bigger profits in your business.

If you would like to see the proper way to offer upsells in action, go to www.sureshmay.com or text your name and email address to 276-565-RICH(7424) and see it live for free!

EIGHT

How to Create an Automatic Sales Machine

The first rule of any technology used in a business is that automation applied to an efficient operation will magnify the efficiency. The second is that automation applied to an inefficient operation will magnify the inefficiency.
– BILL GATES

MILAN, ITALY

SALES WERE MOVING as slowly as cold honey.
Heather's "system" was failing her. She relied on word of mouth and referrals to keep her business alive, but her income was becoming entirely too sporadic.

She became both livid and distressed when she experienced a string of down months in her Eats and Treats restaurant franchise.

Heather was great at creating excitement around her front-end marketing campaigns, but she was terrible at maximizing profits.

She was behind on bills, it was tough to pay her 30 employees, and her stress levels were at an all-time high.

"I don't know how I'm going to come up with payroll this month," Heather said with a shaky voice. She often confided in her mother, Becky, and this time was no different.

Becky had a sharp marketing mind and a great knack for dealing well with people, so she helped Heather through a lot of her business-related problems. Becky had recently been to a *Lifetime Customer Blueprint* seminar in Atlanta where she learned how to tackle these sorts of issues, so she had just the solution.

"Well," Becky spoke with a motherly, reassuring tone, "you have to get more customers in a predictable, reliable fashion."

"How do I do that?" Heather asked.

"You lack a system. That's your first problem. People love your restaurant, but they need something other than 'love' to bring them back in."

Before Heather spoke, she knew her mother was right. Trying to sustain and grow a business on word-of-mouth alone was difficult enough, but without a marketing funnel in place to capitalize off of her previous successes, she was flirting with failure.

"You're right, Mom. I have to go back to the drawing board, and I know what I need to do."

How to Create Your Own Personal ATM

If you've made it this far, you have everything you need to get as many affluent customers as you like, and you know how to make them spend more money.

In this chapter, I'm going to help you put it all together by giving you the secret sales funnel that has done multiple multi-million dollar online and mobile launches.

The most beautiful thing about this system is that once you set it up, it runs on autopilot. Imagine building your digital marketing funnel *once* for it to bring in new customers every day. It's like having your own ATM machine–after it's created, all you have to do is press play to withdraw as much cash as you want.

So how do you create this automated architecture that I call the *Lifetime Customer Formula*?

Read along and watch the digital marketing secrets unfold.

Step 1: Free Lead Generation Offer

A free offer turns people into leads by collecting their interest and allowing you to follow up with them and control the marketing process. The best lead magnet is information your market desires.

Step 2: Welcome or One Time Offer (OTO)

After you acquire a new lead, your main focus is finding out who your buyers are. Qualify your leads with an offer for less than $10. A great welcome offer can be a book, content video, or any kind of low-cost, high-value item.

Step 3: Core Offer

The third step in your million-dollar digital marketing funnel is promoting your main big ticket offer. At this stage of the funnel, you can expect a 30-40% conversion.

Step 4: Upsells and Downsells

Once a customer buys your main offer, you will present another related upsell and a downsell. Your upsell could be an additional high-ticket or continuity product. Upsells are a great way to keep money flowing into your ad spend to generate more leads and sales.

Step 5: Bump Offers

The goal of a bump offer is to increase the order size at the time of checkout.

Step 6: Cross-sell offers

The sixth thing you can implement is a cross-sale.

For instance, if you're selling a diet pill, a natural cross-sale would be a nutritional plan or workout videos.

Step 7: Optional Continuity

The two most popular types of continuity are optional and forced continuity. As their names suggest, optional continuity gives the customer the option to choose whether or not they want to get billed regularly, and forced continuity makes the customer take the option at the time of purchase.

If you have ever purchased Proactiv, you have seen forced continuity at work. When you buy the acne treatment, you are automatically enrolled in bi-monthly billings until you cancel.

Step 8: Back-end offers

Your back-end offers are where you're going to sell super high-ticketed, high-value items and make the bulk of your profits. For instance, I have a $20,000 mastermind group that I offer to highly-leveraged, wealthy entrepreneurs.

Selling high-ticket items can be tricky. To do it effectively, you have to give massive transformational value at premium prices. If done correctly, you will have 10-20% of your customers take action on this offer.

Add these elements to your business and you will unleash the secrets that one of my clients used to launch products and earn over $1.8 million in as little as seven days.

* * *

Heather figured it out. She implemented the *Lifetime Customer Blueprint* formula from start to finish and she could easily predict how much money she would make each month.

More importantly, the guaranteed income from her new "Food of the Month" membership option gave her the capital to expand to four new markets over the next two years.

News and various media outlets helped her restaurant steadily grow, and she soon became a celebrity in the food and restaurant industry.

* * *

What would you do if you became a celebrity? How would that impact your business?

After you read the simple secrets in Chapter 9, you'll be ready to achieve your answer to the previous questions.

Massive Action Items

1. Create Your Own Multi-Million Dollar Marketing Funnel.

Follow the steps in this chapter to outline what your ideal funnel looks like. Creating your ideal funnel will take some work, but the freedom and wealth it provides will be worth it.

If you would like to see this marketing campaign in action so you can implement it for your business, go to www.sureshmay.com or text your name and email address to 276-565-RICH(7424) and get it for free!

Section 3:
How to Make
Customers Buy
More Frequently

NINE

How to Become a Celebrity & Dominate Your Market

Being able to touch so many people through my businesses, and make money while doing it, is a huge blessing.
– MAGIC JOHNSON

AUSTIN, TX

JONATHAN WANTED TO become the highest paid expert in the public speaking industry, but no one really knew who he was.

Over his 10 year career, he spoke at many colleges and various businesses, but he was having difficulty getting past his usual paltry $2,000 per gig fee.

Most of his industry peers felt like that was a major payday, but Jonathan knew he could *do more* and *be more*.

He had a strong message he needed to share

with the world, and he was determined to get it out.

Jonathan didn't have any heavy connections. He didn't have a ton of capital to buy a lot of ads on primetime media.

Jonathan was short in a lot of areas, but with determination and Internet access, he did have one thing: the power to deliver value to the world and make himself famous.

As he realized this, it hit him. He thought to himself, "To get to where I want to go, I have to become a celebrity."

He knew from his *Lifetime Customer Blueprint* training that obtaining celebrity status is the fastest way to multiply your income- and with the right positioning tools in place, it was proven to be easier than he'd thought possible.

Story Selling

Celebrity sells everything–from toys to bedroom sets–having celebrity can catapult you to the upper echelon of your industry. Regardless of what business you're in, you can become and harness the power of celebrity. Becoming a celebrity will allow you to put a WWE choke hold on your competition.

In order for you to do this, you have to lead with your story.

Many people are afraid to tell their unfiltered stories, but your story is going to be one of the most important aspects of your marketing arsenal.

The story gets its power from the trust it creates—when people can feel your bare-boned honesty, they want to connect with and get to know you better.

Even if your story hurts, or if you think it's embarrassing, telling it will make people relate to you faster and easier. When people begin gravitating towards you and your story, this will allow you to become one of the greats and outshine others in your field.

When it comes to selling, a lot of people think that their mastery of the "how to" is the key to being better than their competition. Fortunately, this is not true. If you are playing in a field where everyone is at the top of their game, everyone knows how to do their work well. The "how to" does not really change.

You may have slight variations in strategies, but the fundamentals of how to get a job done usually stay the same.

So how do you differentiate yourself?

You tell your story.

Your experiences, your journey, and your energy will connect with certain segments of the market and *not one* of your competitors will be able to contend with you.

If you have ever listened to my inaugural Art, Ideas, Money + Women podcast, I told the true story of where I started.

I was broke, sleeping in my mother's

boyfriend's basement, and things were not working out. Everything I attempted was producing small results, but I kept pushing and I persevered. After exposing my failures, I transitioned my story to the point in my life where I was building my first seven-figure business.

Days after the podcast aired, I received a bunch of emails from people sharing their stories of failure and triumph, and business owners wanted to work with me because they felt like they knew me.

All of those positive things happened because I was not afraid to be open with my audience and share my personal journey.

After you tell your story, the next step in the Make Yourself a Celebrity plan is to position yourself as an expert and the number one authority in your market.

My mentor and client, Mike Koenigs, taught me his power positioning 10 x 10 x 4 formula. In the 10 x 10 x 4 formula, you create 10 frequently asked questions (FAQ) videos. These will become your money magnets. These 10 videos are designed to put you at the top of the search results for the information your market looks for the most.

The next 10 videos are based on questions that your market *should* ask. When prospects are new to the problems you solve, many won't even know the questions they need to ask for clarity. Answering questions *before* your prospects run into issues quickly positions you as the expert.

Lastly, the remaining 4 videos in the 10 x 10 x 4 formula help with turning your leads into buyers.

Mike is a sharp marketer, so I did what he said—but I took it a step further. I wanted to really establish a dominant presence in the business and marketing world, so I am doing *thousands* of videos.

Every single day I'm shooting ten to twenty pieces of content, and I'm flooding the internet with it. Celebrity positioning is important to me, so I want people to see me everywhere. When people think about business, marketing, sales or leadership, I want them to think about me. I love to serve others and offer value to people's lives, so I want people to come to me with their business questions.

No matter what industry you're in, you can leverage these tactics to become the worldwide go-to person and explode your business.

Illustrate Your Process

How do you do what you do?

Whatever you do to provide your product or service, mapping this out and walking people through your process can prove to be invaluable. Take everything you do to deliver your product or your service and break it down into individual steps.

When you put all of these steps in an illustrated

diagram with a chronological sequence, it shows a high level of expertise, competence, reliability, and it plainly shows buyers the value you're giving them.

This can be worth millions to your business.

Illustrate your process, show people how you do it, and people will know without a shadow of a doubt that you are the expert.

Make Clients Qualify to Do Business with You

Contrary to what most people believe about business, it can be a very profitable idea to turn away clients.

When I bring this point up to an audience, I usually get a unified, "What? Most entrepreneurs and business owners are fighting to stay alive and you're talking about saying 'no' to people who want to pay you!"

It is counterintuitive advice, but take a moment to think about one of the main attributes of celebrity: it is an exclusive club, and exclusivity is profitable.

Capitalizing off of celebrity and making people qualify to do business with you has the ability to erase price and fee resistance. If you are an expert who is hard to get in touch with, you can charge more for your products and services because your limited availability adds value to what is being sold. This alone will give you the ability to charge 10-30x more than your competitors.

Understand What Business You're Really In

More often than not, I find myself in the company of business owners and entrepreneurs. We usually exchange great ideas about marketing and sales, but anytime I ask one of them, "What business are you in?" they respond by telling me their industry.

They may proudly say, "I'm a designer," "I'm a photographer," "I'm a clothier," or "I work in the steel industry."

But they're all wrong.

You are in the *marketing* business.

You are in the business of getting new customers and marketing the thing you sell.

To take it a step further, you are really in *show business*. You want to educate and entertain your market. You want to make people feel good when they're coming into your marketing funnel. You want to constantly deliver value. You want to constantly have an entertainment edge to your business.

Viewing your business this way instantly separates you. A lot of people market their business with the same old dry, boring techniques; these businesses do not give you anything to get excited about.

People love to be entertained. Embrace this fact, and you can make your industry bend to your will.

Borrow Credibility

Another way to quickly catapult you into celebrity is to get borrowed credibility from other celebrities and experts. When you see people taking pictures with celebrities, for example, that's a part of borrowing credibility.

Celebrity photo ops give the impression of, "Hey, I know this guy," even if the reality is that you stood in a line for two hours to take a picture with someone who won't even remember your name.

It makes others think, "Wow! He's associated with someone great. He's associated with someone famous. He looks like he's in the in-crowd. Man, I want to work with him."

Align yourself with other experts and celebrities in your field, and you can be seen as an expert and celebrity, too.

Make Yourself Famous

High-profit clients prefer status over function, convenience, and price. Affluent markets want what's perceived as the best– this means they prefer associating with celebrities, exclusivity, and the most famous businesses.

Making yourself famous begins with pre-framing your customers and creating your legend. The first step in creating your personal legend is determining what you want to be known as.

Do you want to be positioned as a problem solver? How would you like to be known as pioneering and forward-thinking?

For me, part of my legend is becoming known for being very expensive.

I want to be known as someone who has high-priced fees because I understand that high prices equate to a higher value in consumers' minds.

Whatever personal image you want for yourself or your business, this image can easily be cultivated through videos and content.

Celebrities are famous because their faces and their work are displayed on what's called "rock star media." They are on television, the internet, movies, and the radio.

It does not matter how famous (not infamous!) a person is, they became that way from putting out awesome content, and you can do the same thing in your business.

Create insanely good content, proclaim that you are who you want to be, and do everything with confidence and certainty.

Secondly, determine what you want to be known for. Take the time to create and position yourself and your products and services the way you want them to be positioned.

If you want to do big things, *do* big things. Then

tell those stories. Just like rock stars and movie stars, you have to show your stories to people. Send people through the right positioning filter and you can control their perspectives to make people believe what you manufacture.

Also, make sure your aspirations fit your market perfectly. This is one thing that a lot of my clients mess up. You have to understand what your market aspires to become, and you have to understand what they respect and what they like.

We gravitate towards who and what we want to be, so know your market and the results it wants. Become an advocate of the lifestyle your market wants, and people will follow your every lead.

Aligning yourself with the people your market idolizes is a brilliant marketing strategy.

If you know your market wants to have nice clothes, fancy cars, or that they want to be associated with other celebrities, you have to do these things. That's the iconic image that your market aspires to, so sell this idea to them.

You can also reinforce your credibility with pop culture references, the sets and settings you use, and the way you shoot your videos and take your photos.

Like it or not, people believe what they see in videos. When people see pop stars with diamonds and luxury cars, many immediately believe those stars own the items, when in reality they are usually rented. People have become more astute, but it's rare that someone will question the perception you give the market.

If you were tapping into a segment of the market that enjoys flashes of wealth, turn your luxury bravado all the way up!

Again, people believe what they see in videos. That's just how it is.

Even if you start out using the internet, it's just as believable. If you are doing cool stuff in your videos, people are going to believe it.

Now that you know what to do, how should you deliver your content to the market?

Remember this key fact: Celebrities became celebrities because they put out massive amounts of great content.

You can begin with a podcast, a video-cast, you can leverage social media, you can shoot a documentary. There are so many things that you can do to create great content, but the most important thing to do is create *something*.

Content creation can put you in the same arena as your favorite super stars- people love Will Smith because he's in blockbuster movies. Jay-Z has such a huge following because he goes to the studio and records albums.

To achieve these results and get the people to love you, focus on having fun and generating entertaining content for the masses.

BONUS SECRET:

Some of you may be thinking, "This sounds great and all, but how am I going to find the time to create all of this content?"

You don't.

In fact, it's better if the content isn't about you. Take Oprah for example– what is one of the many things she's famous for? She created a platform for other people to publish their content. If you go to Oprah.com, you'll see that she has people guest posting. If you watch her TV show, you'll see that she interviews the top experts and entertainers in every field.

Oprah became famous for interviewing famous people. She positioned herself as an authority, and she has other people furnishing the content.

That's what you want to do in your business.

Use a publishing model. Position yourself as an editor– create the platform, bring on the experts, and you can borrow their credibility to further your goal of making yourself famous and the most credible in your market.

* * *

Jonathan gazed at the stars on the beach resort of his latest speaking gig. He was paid $45,000 to be the main speaker, and everything was all-expenses paid.

He thought about the year before when he was hustling for $2,000 per gig, and he wasn't going back.

All it took was for him to tell his story with passion and enthusiasm, flood the Internet with cool marketing videos, and make businesses qualify to hire him before he accepted speaking jobs. This was the life of a top celebrity public speaker, and he smiled to himself for having the courage to create the exact life he envisioned.

Massive Action Items

1. Create your 10x10x4.

Shoot a minimum of 20 FUN videos that position your business as the best in the world. If you want to do the Frequently Asked and Should Ask questions, you can simply shoot video of yourself answering those questions. As you release these videos to the internet, people searching for the terms contained in your videos will be led back to your site.

2. Determine WHAT you want to be known for and WHO you want to be known as.

Who do you want to be known as? Do you want

to be expensive? I would suggest against it, but do you want to be a low-price leader like Wal-Mart? Do you want to be somewhere in the middle?

If you would like to see my 10x10x4 in action so you can copy the technique (and learn how you can double the sales in your business), go to www.sureshmay.com or text your name and email address to 276-565-RICH(7424) and get the *How to Make More Money Online* video series for free!

TEN

How to Increase Your Sales Conversions

The man who does not work for the love of work but only for money is likely to neither make money nor find much fun in life.
– CHARLES M. SCHWAB

LOS ANGELES, CA

HER SMILEY CAKES cupcakes were the best in town, and just about everyone had tried the delicious treats.

While this was great news, Brittany couldn't get many people to come back to her store.

She had a pretty good in-store experience, but once customers left her business, Brittany never contacted her customers until they came back to the cupcake shop.

This was Brittany's biggest issue because she hadn't taken the time to implement a foolproof follow-up system, and it was costing her in money, customers, and referrals.

Brittany and her staff tried to be as friendly as possible to their customers. It helped, but it wasn't enough to keep them devouring cupcakes.

If she wanted to save her business, she knew it was time to try something simple and incredibly effective.

If you are like Brittany and you haven't found an easy way to consistently follow up and keep in touch with your hard-earned customers, then you will love the lesson that follows.

The Money Is in the Follow-Up

Hands down, the most common question I get from business owners is, "How do I get new customers?"

From the kid with a lemonade stand to Fortune 100 CEOs, everyone wants new customers. If I didn't know any better, I'd think that companies believe new customers are the only way to build a profitable business.

As you learned in the previous sections, there are three ways to grow any business: 1) getting new customers, 2) increasing the average order size, and 3) increasing the frequency of purchase. That's it. All of the fancy things going through your mind fall into one of these three categories.

When it comes to selling and making big bank in your business, what most people don't seem to understand is that the money really and truly is in the *follow-up*.

The easiest (and often most profitable) sales you will ever make will be to current and past customers. Most businesses have a hard time getting new customers, and when they finally do, they rarely make a front-end profit.

If you want to create profitable marketing, the first thing you have to understand is that "one shot" marketing rarely ever works.

One shot marketing is when you promote your business and try to ONLY get the sale the first time you make the offer. This is a terrible strategy for a few reasons, but the most important reason is that most of your customers will not be ready to make a buying decision.

They may not have the disposable cash at the time, you may not have established enough trust, or your offer may not have effectively navigated the sales process.

Whatever their reasons for not buying immediately, you should focus on creating marketing campaigns that have follow-up sequences. After you generate the lead, a follow-up sequence will allow you to convert some of the prospects who did not make an initial purchase.

Additionally, as you follow-up and add value to your leads, you will build more trust and your conversions will increase exponentially over time.

Ask yourself these five tough questions below,

and please be truthful. Answering honestly will only help your business grow.

1. Are you doing a good enough job following up with present and past customers?

2. Are you continuously adding value to customers' lives post-sale?

3. Are you asking customers questions to see how you can continue to serve their needs?

4. Are you building a genuine relationship and rapport with your customers?

5. Are you contacting present and past customers at all?

If you answered "no" to *any one of these questions*, you are leaving *millions of dollars* on the table.

The majority of the profits in your business are going to come from focusing on servicing current and past customers. This is the untapped gold mine of opportunity, and just about ALL businesses miss this mark on some level.

Think about this for a moment: Why focus all of your money and resources on buying new customers instead of opening the vault of profits from the customers you already have?

You probably do not know why.

And that's not OK.

Luckily for you, I'm more than happy to help you implement a system to fix this massive problem right away.

Complicate Your Marketing Strategy

Before we get into the specifics of how to follow up and get more sales, allow me to remind you of this fact: Winning marketing strategies are complicated!

When I first started mastering marketing and sales, I studied *every* marketer's funnel. I'd buy products I didn't need just to envision how I would sell them from an expert's point of view. To this day, I still call TV and newspaper ads to see how those marketers will try to sell me.

When I couldn't afford to buy their products, I'd attempt to copy the visible part of a marketer's funnel. As a novice, I would mimic various landing pages and tweak sales copy to make it my own. And being ignorant of sales psychology, sometimes I'd even straight rip off headlines!

I'd implement other marketers' sales copy and landing pages, and time and time again I'd fail. Why? Because great marketing is deeper than what you see on the surface level.

Master marketing funnels attract customers through a multitude of media sources.

Master marketing funnels create pages and offers based on whether they are targeting warm or cold traffic or not.

Master marketing funnels trigger actions based on a customer's decisions and purchases made from *inside* the funnel.

If you want to make a huge impact on your business and in your customers' lives, you must have a sophisticated, multi-step marketing campaign.

Email Marketing

If you have implemented the steps in this book, you should have driven traffic to your offers and captured a bunch of hot leads! And if you haven't figured it out by now, email is the digital age's primary prospect follow-up tool.

When done correctly, email marketing is capable of helping you serve your customers faster while netting your business millions and millions of dollars in the process!

I recently helped my client Mike Koenigs with his 11th multi-million dollar product launch. This launch grossed $1.8MM in 7 days (with $1MM gross sales on the deadline day), and it was done ALL via email.

You must build up your email list (or get Joint Venture partners to mail for you) to accomplish this level of sales so quickly, but doing so will be easy when you learn the basics.

The most important part of your email is the subject line. Everything I've told you about writing headlines that sell still applies. Your subject line has to be benefit and value-driven. If you fail to pique interest in your subject lines, your prospects won't even bother to open your emails.

After successfully getting your prospects to open an email, be sure to convey a warm, friendly, personal tone throughout. Talk as if you are speaking to a close friend. Anytime I write an email to clients, I keep one of my best friends in mind. This allows me to be conversational, relaxed, and most importantly, my usually fun self.

Even if you were taught in the dead school of "corporate correspondence," stiff and overly professional emails will kill your conversions. We are dealing with *people*, and people do not want to read boring messages. These type of emails lack personality, wit, charm, and the all-important ability to get things sold.

In the email marketing world, there are two different sides colliding. Side A says to offer value in your emails with "selling the click" in mind, while Side B suggests you sell your products and services directly in the body of your email.

I prefer to sell the click, and this is what most of the top digital marketers do. If you are on any good email lists, you will see master marketers make "last minute" offers for sales via email.

Under most circumstances, however, marketers leverage curiosity to get you to click and watch presentations on their websites.

Regardless of your marketing vehicle, repetition trumps everything. Direct mail marketers have known for decades that sending several mailings multiplies your response.

This attitude should be adopted with email marketing as well. The more high-value, story-driven content you send to your list, the more prospects will begin to love and buy from you.

Think about yourself for a second: Every time a company tries to sell you something, you're not always ready to buy. This doesn't necessarily mean that you don't want to buy or that you're not interested in buying, you simply may not be ready to buy at that moment. Your prospects aren't any different, so take this fact into consideration when you are thinking of skipping the creation of a deep and profitable follow-up campaign.

At the end of this chapter, you will have the opportunity to download a free, fill-in-the-blank email template titled "Four Day Cash Machine." It has helped clients make $10,000-$100,000 (or more!) by simply emailing their list of prospects.

Text Message Marketing

There are over 14 billion mobile phones in the world, and there are over 7 billion people.

If you've begun targeting affluent prospects as suggested, your target consumer has a mobile device.

When people receive a text message, they open it. With 100% deliverability and a 97% open rate, It doesn't matter who the text is from- people rarely, if ever, leave unopened messages in their text inboxes.

As a digital marketer, this presents a great opportunity for you.

Picture yourself at a conference or event presenting your products and services to key buyers and decisions makers. Now imagine being able to turn the crowd's mobile phones into your personal marketing funnel that allows you to capture everyone as a lead instantly.

My coaching clients get access to software that allows them to grab the crowd in an instant. Simply put, you'll get a custom phone number or short code such as '58885', and your prospects can text their names and email addresses to be instantly added to your list.

This allows you to build your market share faster than you ever thought possible, and you can get your marketing messages delivered and seen virtually 100% of the time.

Spend More Time Marketing to Current & Past Customers

If you want guaranteed cash, sell to current and past customers- these will be the easiest sales you'll ever make. But why is that? Primarily, because these customers already trust you. They have spent money with you, and if you have great customer service, you have built a great rapport with them by delivering exceptional value.

In every business, your value should extend to the creation of custom-tailored promotions. In a recent poll, 68% of customers said they leave businesses because they feel underappreciated, and another 14% said they switch due to product or service dissatisfaction.

These things are in your control, and there is absolutely no reason you should lose 82% of your customer base due to negligence.

Customized marketing can quickly solve customer dissatisfaction to keep your customers longer. We all love to feel special and appreciated–think about a moment when someone did something nice for you simply to make you smile.

Not only did it likely blow your mind and brighten your day, but you probably wanted to do something nice for them in return.

Investing in customer retention is as simple as serving your customers, making sure your products are up to par, and ensuring that your customers feel appreciated.

For example, if you know that one of your long-time customers, Jan Smith, likes a certain bottle of wine, send her a free bottle every now and then.

This small gestures will pay in spades for a few reasons: When you send prospects one of their favorite things as a gift, it shows that 1) you paid attention to them, and 2) you appreciate them and their business enough to go beyond what they imagined to be excellent customer service.

When you look at your business through this lens, you'll see that simple acts of kindness and a thoughtful follow-up can easily revive and renew old relationships to inspire your clients to commit to you forever. Other gift ideas include personalized greeting cards, thank you cards, coupons for upcoming purchases, and handwritten notes.

These suggestions sound so simple, but hardly anyone does it. When was the last time you wrote a customer a personal note just to say thank you? When was the last time you gave a customer a gift for no reason at all? If your answer is "Never!" or "A long time ago", it's time to change that.

Implement these things. You like to receive gifts and gratitude in your personal life, so think about the effect this will have on customers when you add these touches to your business.

Stick Letters & Bonusing Through the Rebill

Keeping customers from leaving your business is

a big deal. While helping my clients solve their attrition problem, I have them create "stick letters" and free bonus offers to give away when it's time to re-bill customers.

A stick letter works like this: When you sell something, have a special letter in the package offering customers an additional bonus value. This can be a free gift, but whatever it is, just make sure it's exciting enough to make people say, "Wow!" Stick letters will keep people from returning orders and potentially leaving your business.

With "bonus through the re-bill", the tactic is a similar concept. This is usually applied to continuity businesses when it is time for the customer to auto-renew for your product or service. Every 30 days (or however frequently you re-bill your customers), give them something free. This can be anything: high-value, free content, or any low-priced, high-value gift to show your customers your appreciation.

* * *

Brittany created a simple email marketing campaign to keep in touch with everyone who came to her store. She checked her sales from just 30 days prior, and she saw a 75% boost in repeat business.

It's insane how easy it is to retain buyers once you take a vested interest in serving and keeping in touch with your customers.

Brittany discovered this, and with a new desire to consistently serve her current and previous customers, she'd make sure she never lost a customer again.

Massive Action Items

1. Map out your own follow-up sequence.

I'll give you a swipe file to map out your own email follow-up sequence. This email swipe file has helped my clients earn $10,000+ from sending out messages and making offers to via email.

I also want you to brainstorm some fun and creative ways to put a smile on your customers' beautiful faces. These can be gifts, thank you cards, coupons, or personal notes.

If you would like to get the $10,000 "Four Day Cash Machine" email sequence for free, go to www.sureshmay.com/CLCgifts or text your name and email address to 276-565-RICH(7424) and get it now!

ELEVEN

How to Guarantee Your Customers Sell for You

Whether you think you can or whether you think you can't, you're right!
— HENRY FORD

WASHINGTON, DC

A PRIL REALIZED CUSTOMERS loved her chain of flower shops because she provided an excellent product with exceptional service- but none of her customers were spreading the word about her awesome shops.

She ran into one of her long-time customers, Mrs. Cook, on the street one day, and after exchanging some pleasantries, April asked the older woman what she thought the problem was.

Mrs. Cook replied, "Well, April, I stopped telling my friends about your shops because I never received anything for my recommendation. I've sent close to 20 people your way, and not once have I ever received even a simple 'thank you'."

April was shocked to silence. As she listened to Mrs. Cook finish her rant, she realized she'd dropped the ball by not showing her customers appreciation, and she was using the "hope" strategy to get new referrals.

Like most business owners, April assumed that if she gave great service and a great value, people would naturally tell others. This is not always the case, but there *is* a way to guarantee that customers spread your marketing messages.

After April thanked Mrs. Cook for her frankness, she settled with her decision: April was going to implement a company-wide reward system for customers who referred her to others.

It would prove to be one of the most profitable things she ever did.

Refer Your Way to Wealth

One of the fastest ways to organically grow a business and get new customers is through referrals. A referral happens when a current customer tells someone he or she knows about his or her wonderful experiences with your business, leading the current customer's friend or family member to do business with you.

Have you ever had a friend tell you something

positive about a business? If you have, you probably remember feeling the desire to try that business immediately.

Friends' testimonials give businesses more credibility than any advertisement ever could, so it would behoove you to have a plan to make these type of "friend-to-friend" sales take place in your business.

After serving your customers, do you *know* they will refer their friends to your business or do you merely *hope* they will?

If you are still on the "hope and pray" strategy (which, again, is a horrible business plan), allow me to introduce you to the power of having a referral system designed to bring a flood of new customers.

When you're targeting affluent clientele, one of the most important decisions you can make is to focus on attaching experiences and feelings to your products and services.

As you acquire new customers, you don't want your business to be perceived as only a commodity. Commodity businesses compete for customers on price, and these types of businesses are usually positioned as a simple exchange of money for product.

To become a big business that people will love, focus on getting new customers by delivering experiences unlike any other business in the world.

For example, if you're selling a workout

bootcamp and you want more people to come and have a great time, you need to figure out how to make your bootcamp experience so amazing that people will share their excitement with friends.

You might take your group into the woods to jump over rocks, lift logs, climb up trees, do pullups on tree limbs, and jump over shallow streams. After everyone is done, you could have a group of massage therapists give everyone a free massage as a part of your package.

Having people do something differently than going to a gym or a park is noteworthy enough, but if you surprise everyone and give them free massages, you've definitely created something worth talking about!

People are going to remember that, and they are going to tell others about what you are doing.

After you create the excitement, you can take your business to a higher level by selling exclusivity with your experience.

To the wealthy people we are targeting, experience and exclusivity are extremely important. This affluent market will spend almost any amount of money on things that will bring a positive personal change.

You want to make people feel something deep inside; something that makes them come alive.

Achieve this, and you can guarantee that your company will see unprecedented growth.

The persuasive power in offering exclusivity

comes from making people feel unique. If people can buy uniqueness, they will. This is why customers purchase items such inscribed pens, custom tailored clothes, and rare, expensive cars.

Owning these material possessions make buyers feel good because they have something remarkable, something one-of-a-kind.

That's why expensive products and services have such a mass appeal—people want to feel connected and as if they belong—but they also want to feel like individuals who have things others can't attain.

When your focus is getting current customers to share their experiences with potential new clients, these psychological points are important in leveraging your referral marketing strategy.

The E.A.R. Referral Strategy

E.A.R. is an acronym for Earn, Ask, and Reward.

Earn

Before you can even think of having someone tell another person about your business, you must earn that privilege. Earning a referral can mean many things in a business. Here are some of the most common ways to earn a referral:

- Over-deliver and maximize customer value
- Surprise customers with gifts and bonuses
- Solve problems quickly
- Adding exclusivity and experience to your product, removing the importance of price

Take the initiative to out-market your competition by focusing on "wowing" customers and earning more business. Since most business owners take a transactional approach to their business, you can be in a league of your own in no time.

Ask

After you do an incredible job of earning a referral opportunity, you have to ask for the referral. Customers come to a business, make purchases, and ride off into the sunset with no more than a "Come visit us again soon!" from the owner.

Do you remember how you learned to make a great call to action at the end of your ads? The same concept applies here. As soon as your customers display their satisfaction and happiness with your service, ask them this simple 12-word sentence: "Do you know someone else who will be interested in this experience?"

Most happy customers will euphorically say, "Yes! Let me give you XYZ names and numbers."

Ensuring that people give you a referral is *that*

simple.

If you haven't learned by now, I am a junkie for tracking the effectiveness of every aspect of a marketing campaign, and a referral strategy is no different.

Learning specific numbers pertaining to the frequency with which current customers refer new ones is important. To achieve this, you can add tracking codes to your business cards or give referral-only discount codes. This will reveal how effective your referral campaign is, and it will provide the hard data that lets you know what specifics need to be tested to make improvements.

Reward

Referrals are gifts that are usually hard to come by, and you should treat them as such. When customers give you a referral, they're bringing you a brand new business relationship, new profits, and the potential for even more referrals!

A referral is enormously valuable, so be sure to give customers something to make them feel appreciated. It's relationship 101: Treat others as you want to be treated, and they will (normally) continue to spread the love.

Plus, when you give a gift or some sort of thanks, you implement the Law of Reciprocity which makes customers want to continue bringing you new referrals. There are few worse things than a customer sending you a referral and you not taking time to thank them. Simple thanks will take you far, and they can be some of your greatest profit multipliers.

*   *   *

April's referral system tripled her sales over the next three years. She rewarded customers for their referrals, and in turn, her customers rewarded her with their most valuable resource: a stream of consistent, new customers.

Massive Action Items

1. Write the experiences you will offer customers.

Think of the things that impressed you as a customer; the things that made you want to run and tell a friend. Did the company send you a personalized thank you note? Did you get a letter for your birthday? Have you ever received an unexpected gift that made your day? Remember those gestures, and implement them into your business.

2. Plan your incentives for your referral strategy.

What are you going to give the referrer to show your appreciation? What kind of offers or gifts can you give that will not cost you a lot but that have a high perceived value to your consumer?

TWELVE

How to Make Your Customers Buy from You Forever

Motivation is the art of getting people to do what you want them to do because they want to do it.
– Dwight D. Eisenhower

NEW YORK CITY, NY

I HATE SEEING DEAD people," Laura spoke to Michael with a look of disgust. The funeral parlor was dark, the air was dusty, and it reeked of mothballs.

"But my grandad has had this business for decades because it's such a cash cow. I know people are always passing away, but even this business has its highs and lows."

Laura inherited her funeral home from her grandfather, but she had zero intentions of being involved in the business. Laura and her friend

Michael were heavily interested in technology, and they were looking for a way to merge tech with dead bodies.

Michael responded with a puzzled look, "I see. I'm sure there's a way to add a continuity business to this one, but I'm definitely stumped. Naturally, most funeral homes only see customers once," he quipped, "so this will be difficult."

They were both correct, but with a little imagination, even a place where the crowd was *literally* dead can create customers that last a lifetime- or longer.

The Lifetime Customer Blueprint

Imagine getting a customer to your business, providing an excellent product with exceptional service, and keeping that customer for years.

How much would it impact your business if your customers stayed for a year longer?

How about two years? Ten years?

How about if they stayed *forever*?

By following the steps in this book, you will find that getting new customers is relatively easy, but no matter how you slice it, keeping customers coming back to your business is hard.

There are competitors trying to steal them.

Employees and ownership can piss them off.

A bunch of uncontrollable, awful things can

happen.

All things considered (and assuming people want what you are selling), I am going to reveal a way for you to keep your customers buying your product or service forever (or at least for a very long time).

I have been a loyal customer to my hosting, domain, and email marketing companies for years. I have never changed or thought about changing companies. I wouldn't even consider leaving them because another marketer makes a "better" offer.

What's so great about these companies? What makes them special? Why would I not leave even if there is something "better" out there?

What do these companies have in common?

I'll give you a few hints with a couple of stories:

Think about the hair growth brand Rogaine. They supposedly help men rid themselves of the embarrassment of balding hair.

If Rogaine is helping your hair grow back and you stop using the product, what's going to happen? You're probably going to lose your hair again.

When people buy Rogaine, they usually remain Rogaine customers for a lifetime.

Why is that? What is it about Rogaine?

Think about your water bill, light bill, or any of your household utilities. If your water or lights get cut off, you run to pay those bills. You don't think twice about it.

Unless they are dead broke, people never say, "I'll get around to paying my water bill."

If you've ever been behind on a water or light bill, you understand the mad dash of getting the money to those companies as fast as possible.

The thing all of these businesses have in common is one of the most important elements of what I call the *Lifetime Customer Blueprint*.

The *Lifetime Customer Blueprint* is an online coaching program that teaches business owners and entrepreneurs the 12 key elements needed to get and keep customers for life.

In the previous examples, these businesses created what is called a "pain of disconnect".

When you can establish a strong enough pain of disconnect in your business, your customers become *dependent on your product or service*.

They need you to function.

They need you to survive.

They need you to maintain their lifestyles and standards of living.

With a little imagination, *any* business can create a pain of disconnect, and the *Lifetime Customer Blueprint* coaching program will show you exactly how.

The Most Powerful Business Models in the World

Once you learn how to add a pain of disconnect to your business, you'll need to have one of the strong business models below to build a world-class business.

Automatic Recurring Billing

A lot of businesses sell their products to customers once, making it very difficult to sustain a profitable business long-term. Even if you are doing well with a one-time purchase business, you have to find new customers *every single day*.

By adding an automatic recurring billing feature to your business model, you will experience explosive growth and predictable revenue.

It doesn't matter if you re-bill people monthly, quarterly, or yearly, having people continuously pay you will increase revenue quickly and exponentially.

Your cash flow will become predictable, and this will eliminate the worries some businesses face when it comes to having enough positive cash flow to run operations and to serve customers.

Contractual Recurring Payments

Mortgages, rent, and most cellular phone companies have the most powerful business model in the world: contractual recurring payments. If you become creative enough and implement this, not only are you able to bill your customers every month, you'll have a contract to do so.

I started out selling single bottles of my supplement with pay per click and magazine ads, and I discovered the power of continuity billing from one of my mentors.

He said, "Suresh, if you don't have continuity, you don't have a business. If you don't have people paying you every month so you can predict that revenue, you don't have a business. You can sell product one-off, but who wants to get 500 new customers this month and be forced to figure out how you're going to get 500 the next month?"

After I considered his advice for a split second, I was sold. Having customers on an automatic billing cycle is the way to go; if you are doing anything outside of automatic billing, you are playing the game at a disadvantage.

Sell Painkillers, Not Vitamins

When you're trying to create a pain of disconnect and a successful automatic billing feature in your business, sell painkillers instead of selling vitamins.

What does this mean?

Selling painkillers means that you are solving very painful problems for people.

People hate being disconnected from each other, and cell phone companies sell that access.

A lot of men hate their self image when they are bald, and Rogaine sells men the dream of reliving youth by having a full, healthy head of hair.

Hosting and domain companies sell your business access to the internet–without them, you could not do business on your own personal domain.

Software and hardware companies like Apple have an incredible pain of disconnect in their business–if you do not continuously update the versions of your software and hardware, your old products will become obsolete, and that can totally disrupt your end use for the technology. This business model forces you to constantly get new tools– or it will force your technology to quietly go extinct.

This model works because the pain of not having these products and services are usually too great for people to go without. In order to have the best chances of creating a winning, long-lasting business, you MUST sell painkillers.

Vitamin-based businesses are on the opposite end of the spectrum: these businesses may sell cool stuff, but the stuff they sell is not necessarily something customers need to have or keep.

Think about designer clothes. They are cool to have and fun to wear, but you don't necessarily need them. People may or may not buy luxury clothing for a lot of reasons–they may not be able to afford it, they may change their minds about their desire for luxury brands, or they may switch to another brand because a musician made a reference to it in a song.

Whatever their reasons for not continuing to buy from you, it all boils down to a vitamin business having little to no built-in pain of disconnect.

The Top Recurring Billing Models

When you start planning the automatic recurring billing model in your business, you have a few different continuity options to choose from, the most popular being forced continuity, optional continuity, and micro-continuity.

Forced Continuity

If you've ever been automatically enrolled into some kind of monthly billing program, then you've experienced forced continuity. A very famous forced continuity business model is seen in Proactiv.

If you buy a $20 bottle of Proactiv, they automatically enroll you into their bi-monthly billing program in which they charge $40 every two months for a two bottle supply.

When you buy Proactiv, you don't have the

option to say, "I just want one bottle." Being automatically enrolled in the monthly billing program is a part of the offer, and they only want the segment of the market that will comply.

Optional Continuity

Unlike forced continuity, optional continuity gives you an opportunity to opt-out of automatic billing. Many businesses use front-end welcome offers to qualify you as a buyer, and they may immediately ask, "Do you want to get X benefit and enroll in our membership for Y amount of dollars a month?"

Again, you have the option to choose. If you decide to use this type of continuity, your continuity conversions will significantly drop, but your customer satisfaction may be higher than using forced continuity.

Micro-Continuity

The third continuity style is micro-continuity. Forced and optional continuity are perpetual, and sometimes customers leave the program for various reasons when they do not see an end in sight.

Micro continuity solves this problem.

Micro continuity businesses provide customers with an end goal, and this can make customers stay in your billing cycle for a longer period of time.

For example, let's say you are selling an online coaching program for $50 per month. After a while, you learn that customers cancel their billings after the third month.

As a solution to control your attrition and increase the length of time customers stay in your program, you tell them that you have an "8 month online coaching program" instead of just an "online coaching program."

When your customers see that your program has an end, this will make more people commit and stay for the full 8 months. If people were leaving your program at month three, in most cases, implementing this micro continuity will extend your billing cycle for another five months.

Do the math: if people are only staying for three months, you're only making $150 in revenue. If people stay the entire eight months because that's the length of the full program, you will make $400 in revenue. That's an additional $250 in revenue for simply extending your program and giving it a stop date.

Before you decide to choose a micro continuity model, test the other continuity models. If customers are staying in your program for a long time, you do not want to prematurely limit your profits.

Sell Picks and Shovels

Another very powerful business strategy is the idea of "selling picks and shovels" instead of doing the actual work.

This is commonly called *selling* the how-to instead of *doing* the how-to.

Allow your mind to travel back in time to the famous Gold Rush. If you're a youngster reading this book, the Gold Rush was when many Americans were rushing out West towards California to strike it rich from digging gold.

Many people packed up their hopes and dreams to stake everything they had on making "easy money," but the only people who really got rich were those selling the picks and shovels to do the digging.

A lot of the people who did the actually digging died making that journey. Others spent their fortunes trying to get rich, and ended up broke.

The people that were there selling tools, ideas, and information to people trying to "dig and get rich" became enormously wealthy.

In your business, try to sell picks and shovels for anything your customers tell you they want. Sell the tools, and let your customers do the work.

The Profitable Language of Membership

When you want to get people to become lifetime customers, you should also have a membership aspect to your business. To pull a membership off, you need to have an aspirational identifier that many people want. There also needs to be elite, exclusive access and privilege for members only.

The most popular memberships in the world are exclusive. Exclusivity intensifies people's desire to join your organization because it makes them feel like they are important.

Rich and successful people want to associate with other rich and successful people, and people who aspire to be like them will normally go to any lengths to be seen amongst the elite.

How to Sell Continuity Business Models

The best way to sell continuity programs is to actually *not* try to sell people on the continuity.

What do I mean by this? If you're having difficulty getting customers into your auto-billing membership, you should focus on selling a front-end offer and attach your continuity to it.

For example, consider *Sports Illustrated*. When *Sports Illustrated* sells magazines, they don't actually try to sell you on a magazine subscription.

Sports Illustrated may lead with a t-shirt, a football phone, or even a sexy swimsuit calendar. Once you get this front-end item free plus shipping and handling, they give you a 60-day trial of *Sports Illustrated*.

That's one of the biggest secrets in the marketing game: Do not try to sell continuity.

People do not like making long-term commitments to pay bills, so give away the continuity as a trial.

Keep Your Offers Fresh

In order to get as many people as possible into your new membership program, you need to keep a fresh front-end offer.

Sports Illustrated may run an offer for a football phone one month, a swimsuit calendar the next month, a t-shirt after that, and then a fleece jacket after that. All of these things will be attached to a free trial subscription of the magazine, and they're always switching the front-end offer because you never know what will be the biggest appeal for your target audience.

Everyone you targeted may like sports, but everyone is not going to be pulled in by every front-end offer.

* * *

After weeks of thinking it over, the idea hit Michael like a ton of bricks. One day over dinner, he startled Laura when he screamed, "I got it!"

"What?" Laura jumped, excited. She was excited because though she didn't know what to expect, she knew Michael's idea would blow her away.

"I know what we can do to add a pain of

disconnect continuity model to the funeral home."
Michael could barely contain himself. "We can
partner with an online flower service to have fresh
flowers taken to the tombs and headstones every
week. Many clients don't have time to get out to
the gravesites to do it, and some don't like to visit
at all."

Laura listened intently to the brilliant plan.

She loved it.

Then she butted in, "We can charge a monthly
fee for the service, and because it's a loved one
who passed away, it's very likely that they will
keep the service forever! No one would like to *stop*
sending fresh flowers to something as personal and
emotional as a gravesite! I like the way you think,
Mike!"

They high-fived each other, shared big smiles,
and happily finished their meal.

Anything is possible with a little imagination.

Massive Action Items

1. Brainstorm continuity products and decide on the ideal recurring billing model for your business.

What can you sell on a monthly, bi-monthly, quarterly, or yearly basis? This can be anything, but the fastest product that you can get to market will be an information product. Focus your thoughts on products that your target market will want renewed often.

How to Achieve Your Biggest Goals & End Rich

To succeed... You need to find something to hold on to, something to motivate you, something to inspire you.
– TONY DORSETT

fall 2013 by SURESH MAY

I STARTED OUT BROKE.
I've been homeless, foodless, and penniless.

In my early twenties, I spent many nights unable to sleep because I did not have a clear vision about what I wanted to do with my life.

One day after being fed up, I wrote a simple goal on a piece of paper. At the time, it seemed almost unbelievable to me. This was the goal: I want to make $5,000 in monthly income in 30 days. Exactly 31 days later, I had two consulting contracts valued at $5,200 per month helping business owners increase sales and improve marketing.

With that experience, I've learned that this one thing trumps everything else: Your ability to set BIG goals and make plans to achieve them is the MOST IMPORTANT SKILL TO MASTER.

Three things directly determine your business's success: how big you set your goals, whether or not you take action, and if you have the courage to persist through the trials and the failures.

Brian Tracy wrote, "The higher and more challenging the goals you set for yourself, the more disappointment and adversity you will experience."

Florence Shinn says, "Every great work, every big accomplishment, has been brought into manifestation through holding to the vision, and often just before the big achievement comes apparent failure and discouragement."

To get everything you want in your life, you have to learn to follow directions and take action. Here is your first requirement: Stop reading these words, go get a pen and a pad, and return to read the following 3 step action plan to help you set BIG GOALS and CRUSH THEM!

Action Item #1: Think Big, Start Big, and ASK to GET

When setting your goals, it is essential to set your sights AS HIGH AS YOU CAN POSSIBLY

IMAGINE. Most people set their goals too low because they *think* that's all they can accomplish.

First, think about what you TRULY want: a billion dollar a year business? Then set your sights on a billion dollars. Do you want a business that is automated so you have the free time to travel the world? Then set that as your goal.

Being honest with yourself and setting MONSTER goals is important because there is one thing I can guarantee: If your goal is not big enough, if the reward from your toils is not great enough, you will not create the excitement and enthusiasm needed to help you overcome the obstacles that will inevitably stand in your way.

The second reason thinking big and setting big goals are important is because it dictates whether or not you START BIG.

For instance, when I created my *Lifetime Customer Blueprint* coaching program, my first goal was to create $100,000 in monthly recurring income. To achieve this goal, I had to help and sell memberships to 1,493 people.

This is not a small number, but since I knew that I REALLY wanted to make $1,000,000 in residual income per month from the coaching program, it was not large enough. I was thinking too small.

To sell 1,493 people into a membership program can be done in a relatively short period of time by cold-calling, running small ads, and if you have a targeted list, sending them offers.

With the exception of the low one-to-one leverage offered by cold calling, these methods of marketing offer a decent amount of leverage, but they were not sufficient enough to help me reach my goals in the time I set to achieve them.

When I was honest with myself about making $1,000,000 per month by selling 14,926 memberships, I INSTANTLY began thinking about bigger ways to market and add more powerful forms of leverage.

In the time I set to achieve this goal, the methods I thought to use for achieving the smaller goal would not offer enough speed and leverage.

I began to think about creating JV deals, affiliate relationships, and partnering with other people who had big distribution lists of people from my target market.

I began thinking of using Other People's Money (OPM), Other People's Time (OPT), and Other People's Influence (OPI) so I could borrow their credibility, endorsements, and celebrity to help me reach my goals FASTER and with LESS EFFORT.

When you are honest about the big goals you want to set, your thinking will guide you in the direction to accomplish everything you desire.

Finally, you have to ASK to GET. If you want something, ASK for it. This is deceivingly simple, because most people are too afraid to ask for what they want.

Think about it: When we fear hearing a "no", we rarely ask for what we want *because* of that fear. We usually have the losing battle with failure in our minds and we never even try.

I'm sure you can think of hundreds of times this happened to you. Or how about this: You really want something big, but you ask for significantly less than what you want. You may even ask for less than what you think you're worth.

When it comes to asking for what you want, it's important to understand three things: people will usually say yes, people will usually give you what you asked for, and people judge you based on your requests.

If you ask someone for the moon and stars, not only are you more likely to get them, but people will respect you more because they can tell you mean business. Inversely, if you ask for little, you will usually get it, but people will oftentimes lose respect for you because you do not seem to value yourself and your product/service/skills as much.

Make it a habit to ask for more than what you want. You'll be surprised at how often you get it.

Action Item #2: Define Your Major Goals & Objectives

After you THINK BIG, START BIG, and understand that you MUST ASK FOR WHAT YOU WANT, it will be time to write down your major goals and objectives.

First things first: WHY do you want to achieve your goals? What's fueling you? Will your current goals inspire you to keep going when you run into obstacles and setbacks?

Maybe you want to achieve a goal because it will help you take care of your family. Maybe you want to accomplish a goal so you can be financially secure. Maybe you want to be a celebrity and have influence in other people's lives. Whatever your reasons, write them down! This is an important step because it keeps that burning desire strong during those hard to endure days.

There is a ton of power in committing your goals to paper. When you commit aspirations with deadlines to paper, they instantly go from dreams to goals that can be accomplished.

When you write your goals on paper, be sure to make them as clear and as detailed as possible. The details will show you every step that needs to be taken in order to achieve your goal.

For instance, say your goal is to write a high-converting sales page. Within this major goal, there are a lot of smaller goals that must be completed before tackling the main goal.

In order to write compelling copy that sells, you have to study your market to find out its wants, needs, and frustrations. If you are a beginner, you may need to study copywriting basics. You should probably study other sales letters that have sold millions of dollars worth of products and services to see the elements of great copy. This process will be great for revealing any big obstacles that have to be completed before moving forward.

Detailing your goals will also reveal whom you need on your team. If you want to build a web-based business and you do not know how to hack web pages, you will need to hire a designer and a coder.

If you are using direct response marketing to get new leads and customers, you will need to have a clear vision of your customer acquisition costs, how much you are willing to spend to get each new customer, and how much revenue you need to generate to make direct marketing efforts profitable.

Then, you MUST set deadlines for your goals. A goal without a deadline is still a wish. A deadline forces you to check your progress, be accountable for your actions, and measure your progression.

Another important note on goals: write them as if you've already completed them. Most people, if they write their goals at all, write them as things they *will* do or *want* to accomplish. This isn't a good practice. Your goals should be written as "I am...", "I earned...", "I accomplished...", etc.

Below are examples of good goals versus a bad goals:

Bad:

"I will earn a residual income of $5,000 per month with my product."

Excellent:

"I EARN a residual income of $5,000 per month by selling my product/service. This goal was completed by X date."

Bad:

"I will write a sales letter."

Excellent:

"I wrote a sales letter for X market. I wrote X pages/words per day until it was completed by X date."

Bad:

"I want a new car."

Excellent:

"I drive a new Ferrari 458 Spider. It is red with a peanut butter tan leather interior. I sold/marketed/ created X to get this car, and I have this car on or before X date."

Be specific with what you want. Recite your goals at least twice a day, envision yourself having, being, and doing what you want. You'll see that you can double your sales, improve your life, and achieve all of your goals faster than you ever thought possible!

Action Item #3:
Make an ACTION Plan!

The third and final action item in this 3-step action plan is to make YOUR action plan! After you decide on your BIG goals, get clear on why you want to achieve those goals.

Write your goals down with specifics, and envision yourself as already having completed your goals; you must then make precise daily action steps to accomplish your chief objectives.

To accomplish your goals in the fastest time possible, you should commit to doing something everyday. You should have a clear way of tracking your goals to review your progress and stay on course.

Under Action Item #2 I gave an example goal: Create a web-based business.

Depending on what you are selling, your website could take days, weeks, or months to create, and you have many sub-goals and milestones that have to be met before the project will be completed.

You have to write sales copy, get product images, code web pages, get a shopping cart checkout system, get a merchant account to process credit cards, create a marketing funnel, and write ads to drive traffic.

These are just a few sub-goals that have to be completed before you can have an active web-based business, and each one has its own action items to ensure finalization.

Under your main goal, list out each of its sub-goals. After that, take one or two of the objectives from the sub-goals and make them your daily action items.

Over time, you will easily be able to track what you have done and which sub-goals still need to be completed before crossing off your major goals.

Tracking your goals this way will also explicitly illustrate if you are holding yourself accountable, or dropping the ball.

After you create your list of major goals and sub-goals, prioritize the list into two separate parts: the important things that make money and the important things you should outsource that would take up too much of your time.

Outsourcing your goals will add speed and leverage to achieving what you want.

Outsourcing is also valuable for another practical reason: You SHOULD NOT do everything yourself!

As a business owner, it is important for you to

focus on profit activities as much as possible.

If you can afford to outsource all busy work, DO IT. Nothing slows you down more than doing things that someone else can do faster and better than you.

Even if you create the perfect plan to achieve your goals, you will encounter setbacks and you should expect to fall short initially.

Failure is natural in the beginning. When we start something new, we have no idea what to expect, and we usually don't have all of the necessary skills we need to master.

When you hit these inevitable walls, adjust your goals and PERSIST! Persistence is the key to getting everything you want. If your "why" is strong enough, you should have no problem persevering through the struggles in getting all you desire.

Whatever you set your sights on, I believe you can do it. In fact, since I believe in you so much, I'll put my money where my mouth is: To learn how you can use the secrets I used to accomplish my goals of getting endorsement deals and testimonials from Olympic Gold medalists, NBA and NFL athletes, and the #1 female MMA fighter in the world, go to http://www.sureshmay.com/goalsbonus to get the free guide that will show you exactly how to CRUSH your big goals!

Afterword: The Final Chapter Before Your Business Breakthrough

What a ride!

I know that you are pumped up, excited, and ready to take action.

So now what do you do?

Well, like all of the stories I shared in this book, the most important thing for you to do at this very moment is to take massive action.

I know you want to create your own digital marketing ATM-styled "money machine", so you must put everything you've learned into effect.

When you do take action, you'll discover heights you've never imagined. You'll discover a power in your business as you've never witnessed before.

I have helped clients do $1,800,000 product launches in as little as seven days and create #1 best-selling books the *instant* the book was launched. I'd love to help you create a digital marketing campaign as well.

Your transformational experience can begin one of two ways:

You can go to www.sureshmay.com/LCB and get additional *free* deep-dive training for my *Lifetime Customer Blueprint* online coaching program. This simple, step-by-step program will give you instant access to the specifics that will help you get new business *immediately*.

The *Lifetime Customer Blueprint* coaching program will take you and your business to a place that you've never been before, and the journey will be amazing.

Again, that's www.sureshmay.com/LCB.

If you would prefer to work with me directly, go to www.sureshmay.com/qualify to see if we are a good fit to work together to catapult your business into outer space!

The best thing you can do to take advantage of this high is to *take massive action*. I'm looking forward to hearing from you, so let's get started.

www.sureshmay.com/qualify

Suresh May
Jetton Group LLC
July, 2014

Acknowledgements

First, I have to thank the spirit of action, discipline, consistency and commitment that has allowed me to complete this work of literary art.

To my sister and brilliant editor, Jasmine S. McGowan Your mastery with a pen transformed my art from potential to extraordinary like the glass slipper did Cinderella. Thank you, and here's to many more!

To my son, Syre J. May Your presence, huge smile, and jovial laughter help me push through the dark days. You inspire me to go harder for greatness because I know you're watching my every move.

Shirley McGowan Thank you for supporting and helping me even when you didn't quite understand my vision. You are the epitome of love, generosity, and sacrifice. I love you dearly, and I'll take care of you forever.

Brian Johnson I thank you for helping me stay on track, accountable for my actions, and for being a guiding light for greatness. You've helped me every step of the way on my entrepreneurial journey, and for that I'm eternally thankful. Anyone would be honored to call you a friend, and I get to call you one of my best.

Mike Koenigs You granted me the opportunity that changed my life in a flash. I'll cherish your guidance, giving spirit, and expert mentorship until the end of my days. You have inspired me beyond belief, and you are hands down one of the best in the industry.

Greg and Linda Edwards Thank you for opening your home to me and giving me the tools that helped me on my journey to become a master in sales and marketing.

Aisha Baker Thank you for always being supportive, kind, and giving. I'll always cherish you.

Donald May I've been blessed to have you as an uncle/father-figure/mentor. I'm thankful for the way you always supported and believed in me.

Martin Smith Without you, I could've been homeless. I thank you for your kindness, patience, and support on my road to greatness.

Lastly, if you've ever helped me in any way, I thank you from the bottom of my heart. My only wish is that I have added as much value to your life as you have to mine.

On that note, I want to give a personal mention to a few other people:

Shauncy Davis, Ashley Minns, Roxanne Thomas, Dontell Jefferson, Kerry Sandifer, Julius Gresham, Mark Cooper, Jason Hughes, Steven Rodney, Andrea Wilder and the Wilder family, Amanda Green, Iesha Kelley, Terrica Phillips, Josephine Reed, Kisha Walker, Yava Jones-Hall, Rashaad May, Gloria May, Patricia May, Hassan May-Riggs, Mary May, Erica May, Kendria May, Amy May, Takova Wallace, Daryl Minor, Delanyard Robinson, Barbara Robinson, Amber Saunders, Zada Summers, Gloria Ward, Aseelah House, Kevin Wales, Kevin Jones, Jr., Kevin Jones, Sr., Latonya Jones, Lorraine Farr, Scott Gilbert, Monique Stancle, John Francis, Joyce Owens, Johnson Cook, Heather Heckel, DeVera Long, Jessica Long, Demetria Griffin, Greg Thompson, Jason Coleman and family, Arthur Talley, Jr., Arthur Talley, Sr., Corrine Talley, and the entire Talley family.

ABOUT THE AUTHOR

Suresh May, artist and serial entrepreneur, has been featured on ESPN and countless radio shows and podcasts. He is the originator of the *Art, Ideas, Money + Women* podcast. He runs a digital marketing, publishing, and software firm from wireless locations worldwide, and he loves painting, drawing, reading, exercising, goofing off with his awesome son, and discussing world-changing ideas with brilliant people. At the time of publication, Suresh is 30 years old.

If you are interested in having Suresh address your organization, or if you wish to receive more information about his *Lifetime Customer Blueprint* program, books, and courses, send an email to info@sureshmay.com.